PROMISES, PROMISES
God Always Keeps His Promises
For Victorious Living Now

Angeline L. Williams

**Promises, Promises.
God Always Keeps His Promises
For Victorious Living Now**

Copyright © 2021 Angeline L. Williams

ISBN-13: 978-1-7325258-2-5

Published by Redemption Books
www.redemptbooks.com
This title and other titles by author are available for quantity discounts for sales promotions, gifts, and evangelism. Visit our website or email us.

All rights reserved. No portion of this publication may be reproduced, stored in a retrieval system, or transmitted in any form or by any means, electronic, mechanical, photocopy, recording, scanning, or other except for brief quotations in printed reviews, without written permission of the publisher.

Book Design: Williams DocuPrep — www.williamsdocuprep.com

Unless otherwise noted, scripture quotations are taken from the New King James Version®. Copyright © 1982 by Thomas Nelson. Used by permission. All rights reserved.

Scripture quotations marked (NLT) are taken from the Holy Bible, New Living Translation, copyright © 1996, 2004, 2007, 2013, 2015 by Tyndale House Foundation. Used by permission.

Scripture quotations marked (ESV) are taken from The Holy Bible, English Standard Version®, copyright © 2001 by Crossway, a publishing ministry of Good News Publishers. Used by permission.

Scripture quotations marked NIV are taken from The Holy Bible, New International Version ®. Copyright© 1973, 1978, 1984, 2011 by Biblica, Inc.™. Used by permission of Zondervan.

Table of Contents

Introduction 3
Your Covenant Right 10
    Practice Exercise #1: 22
Promise Maker, Promise Keeper 26
Activating the Promises 41
Watch Out For Those Snares 54
    Prayer for Spiritual Attack: 59
Pray After 60
This Manner … 60
    Keys To Answered Prayer 68
    Practice Exercise #2: 74
Stand on God's Promises 82
Scripture Promises 88
    Guidance and Help 89
    Practice Exercise #3: 92
    God's Goodness 94
    Practice Exercise #4: 95
    For Healing 98
    Practice Exercise #5: 102
    Protection 104

- Practice Exercise #6: 106
- For Prayer 108
  - Practice Exercise #7: 112
- Strength And Power... 114
  - Prayer Confession for Strength And Power 117
  - Practice Exercise #8: 118
- For Provision... 121
  - Prayer for Provision 125
  - Practice Exercise #9: 126
- For Times of Doubt... 128
  - Practice Exercise #10: 131
- For Impatience... 133
  - Practice Exercise #11: 135
- For Times Of Persecution 137
  - Practice Exercise #12: 139
- For Times Of Grief 141
  - Practice Exercise #13: 144
- For Times of Loneliness.. 146
  - Practice Exercise #14: 149
- For, Stress, Worry and Anxiety................................. 151
  - Practice Exercise #15: 155
- When Things Get Tough 157
  - Practice Exercise #16: 161
- My Prayer for You... 163
- Notes.. 166
- About The Author.. 170

Introduction

"God is not a man, that He should lie, Nor a son of man, that He should repent. Has He said, and will He not do? Or has He spoken, and will He not make it good?" —Numbers 23:19

There are thousands of promises from God in the Bible. Some of them God made to certain individuals, so which promises are for you? Well, if you're a Believer in Jesus Christ, all of them belong to you.

"According as his divine power hath given unto us all things that pertain unto life and godliness, through the knowledge of him that hath called us to glory and virtue" —2 Peter 1:3

God's promises are either unconditional or conditional, positive, or negative. God has promised eternal life to everyone who will believe on Jesus and accept Him as Lord and Savior.

John 3:16 says,

> "For God so loved the world that He gave His only begotten Son, that whoever believes in Him should not perish but have everlasting life."

The promise is that we will receive eternal life, but only if we believe in Jesus. This is both a positive and conditional promise. God has also promised eternal damnation to those who don't obey the Gospel (2 Thessalonians 1:8-9). Being shut out from the presence of the Lord and everlasting destruction definitely negative. I can't imagine anyone would want that.

An unconditional promise is guaranteed with no "ifs" or strings attached on our part, such as the promise God made to Noah after the flood (Genesis 9:11-13) or the promise of Jesus' return (Luke 12:40). The manifestation of this promise does not depend on anything we do.

Then there are conditional promises that require action on our part, such as the promise Jesus made in Matthew 6:33 says,

> "But seek first the kingdom of God and his righteousness, and all these things will be added to you."

All these things refer to God's provision. The condition is to put God first in your life and seek the things that will glorify Him then these things shall be added to you.

Some promises we must ask for such as the promise of wisdom in James 1:5 which says,

> *"If any of you lacks wisdom, let him ask of God, who gives to all liberally and without reproach, and it will be given to him."*

And in Psalm 37:4 which says,

> *"Delight yourself in the Lord and He will give you the desires of your heart."*

God has promised to give us the desires of our heart when we delight in Him. Delighting yourself in the Lord is choosing to live yielded to God. We delight in the Lord when we are obedient to His will (1 Samuel 15:22, Psalm 40:8).

Another conditional promise is in Proverbs 3:5-6 which says,

> *"Trust in the LORD with all thine heart; and lean not unto thine own understanding. In all thy ways acknowledge Him, and He shall direct thy paths."*

Imagine your entire life being directed by the True and Living God who holds the entire universe in place. To acknowledge God all our ways we must recognize Him as the Supreme authority. We must admit His word is true and respond to it.

Even though some promises were made to specific people, like the promise God made to Joshua which says,

> *"No one will be able to stand up against you all the days of your life. As I was with Moses, so I will be with you; I will never leave you nor forsake you."* —Joshua 1:5

Because of what Jesus did on the Cross, Believers today can stand on that promise and all the promises of God. 2 Corinthians 1:20 tells us,

> *"For all the promises of God in Him are Yes, and in Him Amen, to the glory of God through us."*

Since we are in Jesus and no man can stand against Him, no man can stand against us. Unfortunately, very few of us believe God's promises are for them, so they don't access God's promises.

Our knowledge and understanding of our identity in Christ is crucial to the Christian life. The primary way to get this knowledge and understanding from the word of God. The Bible says Satan comes to steal the word (Luke 8:12). He does this because he doesn't want you to know your true identity. He doesn't want you to live in the freedom found in an identity in Christ. The primary tool we have that Satan tries to discredit Satan's lies is the Word of God.

I believe this is why there is so much controversy regarding the Word itself and speaking and confessing the Word of God, especially on the internet. Sadly, many who speak against praying and declaring scripture are Christians.

They believe declaring and confessing the Word of God is unbiblical, and an attempt to manipulate God.

Like Saul, they do not realize that it is the very Word of God that they are coming against. Saul thought he was doing God's work, but he was deceived. It wasn't until Jesus came to him, and taught him the truth, that the eyes of is his understanding were opened (Acts 9:4). There are so many religions among us today, all vying for our soul. Some selectively use Christian words, but not the truth of the Gospel.

Yes, there are erroneous teachings regarding praying and confessing the Word of God, and yes, there are some who have taken God's word taught it incorrectly, but man's error does not mean God's error. God himself has said we should keep His Word on our lips.

> *"8 This Book of the Law shall not depart from your mouth, but you shall meditate in it day and night, that you may observe to do according to all that is written in it. For then you will make your way prosperous, and then you will have good success. —" Joshua 1:8*

The scripture says do not let God's word depart from your mouth. In other words, speak it, declare it, and confess it continually. It says you shall meditate in it day and night. To meditate means to focus one's thoughts on, to reflect on, ponder over, think deeply and carefully about something.

Another way to meditate on God's Word comes from the Hebrew word for meditation: *'hâgâh,'* which means to utter, muse, study, speak the words of the text over and over to yourself. This helps us memorize the verses. Also, as we meditate on God's Word, He will open our understanding and bring revelation knowledge on the passage so we can apply it to our daily life.

God wants us to study His Word, and dig into the passages so, when you read the scriptures, don't just breeze through the words, meditate on what it says. See how it applies to your daily life, and if there is something we don't understand, ask questions, seek answers (Matthew 7:7-8). If you don't understand and believe the Word of God, you cannot follow it.

The scripture says to make it your intent to walk according to all you have learned. Manifestation of the promises follow obedience. The scripture goes on to say then YOU will make your way prosperous, not God, and then you will have good success. Success is the will of God. We can take every thought captive into the obedience of Christ by speaking the word of God.

Psalm 1:2-3 says,

> *"But his delight is in the law of the Lord; and in his law doth he meditate day and night. And he shall be like a tree planted by the rivers of water, that*

bringeth forth his fruit in his season; his leaf also shall not wither; and whatsoever he doeth shall prosper."

Knowing, believing, and standing on the promises of God can help us navigate our daily lives, and overcome fear, temptation, and danger. The Bible is full of God's promises! Too many to mention here. The promises of God cover every area need or challenge we will ever face. Whether you need emotional healing, wisdom, guidance, provision, protection, or whatever you need there are promises that cover it. You can pray one of God's promises that relates to your issue, and hold on to it.

Promises, Promises. God Always Keeps His Promises is the companion to my book Put the Word in Your Mouth. I have received several wonderful testimonies from people who have read the book and applied the message to their life how their life has changed. If you haven't read it, I encourage you to get it and read it along with this book and your Bible. I pray this message stirs your faith, and helps you cultivate a habit of speaking what God speaks, and helps to deepen your prayer life and your love for God's Word.

> *"And now, O LORD God, confirm forever the word that you have spoken concerning your servant and concerning his house, and do as you have spoken." —*
> *2 Samuel 7:25*

Your Covenant Right

When you gave your heart to Christ you became a citizen of the Kingdom of God. As a Believer (a child of God) you have certain undisputable rights because of the covenant between Jesus and God, signed in Jesus' blood. A covenant is an agreement between two parties. If Jesus is your Lord, then you are in right-standing with God. You have been made righteousness through Christ and you have a right to everything God has.

The Bible says in Galatians 4:7, *"Thou art no more a servant but a son."* A son has rights that servants don't have. A son is privy to information regarding his father's kingdom that servants are not. As a citizen of the Kingdom of God you have a covenant right to everything in the Kingdom. You are a recipient of the covenant between Jesus and God, signed in Jesus' blood.

How you see God, knowing and understanding who you are in Christ, what belongs to you and your spiritual authority is an important key to an effective prayer life. Who is God to you? How do you see God? Knowing God is much more than knowing of Him. What you believe about God determines how you see God. What you believe God thinks about you determines how close you will grow toward Him.

Do you believe God causes human suffering? Do you believe you are unworthy of being blessed by God, that nothing good will ever come to you? Do you think sickness, natural disasters, and calamities are God's way of punishing us, that God is angry with us or against us? Thinking this way can cause you to react to God out of fear, and bitterness, or even resentment. It can keep you from truly accepting God's forgiveness and from receiving His blessings. It will keep a Believer who is victorious through Christ living a defeated life.

Scripture says Jesus delivered many who were demon possessed, and he drove out the spirits with a word and healed all the sick (Matthew 8:16).

> *"23 Jesus went throughout Galilee, teaching in their synagogues, proclaiming the good news of the kingdom, and healing every disease and sickness among the people. 24 News about him spread all over Syria, and people brought to him all who were ill with various diseases, those suffering severe pain, the demon-possessed, those having seizures, and the paralyzed; and he healed them." —Matthew 4:23-24*

Why would Jesus heal and deliver people if deliverance and sickness and suffering were sent from God as a punishment? (Matthew 4:23-24)?

> *"Therefore, if the Son makes you free, you shall be free indeed." – John 8:36 (NKJV)*

According to scripture all Believers have been raised with Jesus and are seated with Him in the heavenly realms.

> *"5 Even when we were dead in sins, hath quickened us together with Christ, (by grace ye are saved;) 6 And hath raised us up together, and made us sit together in heavenly places in Christ Jesus:" –Ephesians 2:5-6 KJV*

We are in Christ, far above all principalities and powers of darkness now. Of course, Satan does not want you to settle this in your heart. He doesn't mind if you read it or hear it, but he does not want you to live by it, because then you will exercise your authority over him. Evil spirits can't influence Believers who live seated in Christ! Seated in Christ is a position of authority, honor, and triumph—not failure, depression, and defeat.

> *"If then you were raised with Christ, seek those things which are above, where Christ is, sitting at the right hand of God. Set your mind on things above, not on things on the earth. For you died, and your life is hidden with Christ in God." —Colossians 3:1-3*

There is a story about a farmer who found an eagle's egg and brought it home to his chicken coop. I've read many versions of the story, and maybe you have too, but I want to share my version.

So, when the egg hatched, the young eagle only saw chickens around him. Not knowing what he truly was, he mimicked what he saw around him. He believed he was a chicken, so he lived like a chicken. He scratched, pecked, and flew short distances.

One day a preacher came to the chicken farm to see if what he had heard about an eagle acting like a chicken was true. The preacher knew that eagles symbolize freedom, strength, and power so he was surprised to see the eagle strutting around, acting like a chicken.

The farmer explained to the preacher that this bird was no longer an eagle. He was now a chicken because he had been trained to be a chicken and he believed that he was a chicken. Knowing that the bird was born an eagle and had the heart of an eagle, and nothing could change that the preacher lifted the eagle onto the fence and said, "Eagle, you are an eagle. You have been given great ability to soar above, not pluck and scratch beneath. Stretch forth your wings and fly."

The eagle moved slightly, only to look at the man; then he glanced down at the chickens in the chicken coop and jumped down and continued doing what chickens do. The farmer was said, "See I told you it is a chicken now."

The preacher came the next day trying to convince the farmer and the eagle that the eagle was born for something greater. He took the eagle to the top of the farmhouse and spoke to him: "Eagle, you are an eagle. You have been given great ability to soar above, not pluck and scratch beneath. You belong to the sky and not to the earth. Stretch forth your wings and fly." The large bird looked at the man, then again down into the chicken coop. He jumped from the man's arm onto the roof of the farmhouse.

Not wanting to give up, the preacher asked the farmer to let him try one more time. He would return the next day and prove that this bird was an eagle. The farmer convinced otherwise, said, "Okay, but I'm telling you it is a chicken now."

The preacher realized that if he changed what the eagle saw he could see who he really is. So, he returned the next morning to try again. This time he took the farmer and eagle to the foot of a high mountain where they could not see the farm nor the chicken coop. The preacher then held the eagle on his arm and pointed high into the sky toward the sun, and said: "Eagle, you are an eagle. You have been given great ability to soar above, not pluck and scratch beneath. You belong to the sky and not to the earth. Stretch forth your wings and fly."

This time the eagle looked into the sky and the bright sun straightened his body, and slowly stretched out his wings. As he stretched out his massive wings, he realized he could do it. He moved his wings with a little more power and with the mighty screech of an eagle, flew up and began to soar as he was created to do.

So many Believers live with a chicken mentality. They are saved and equipped to produce greatness and to reach maximum levels of success, but because all they see is their past mistakes and experiences, they can't move outside the coop, and as a result, they live beneath their capabilities. Not only that, but they either don't know their spiritual authority, or they know about it, but don't know how to use it. So, they stop short of achieving the victory God has already given them.

Salvation is about so much more than going to heaven. Salvation literally means deliverance, preservation, pardon, restoration, healing, wholeness and soundness. You were created in the image of the Almighty God to rise above and soar like an eagle. If Jesus is your Lord, each of the following statements is true about who you are in Christ, what belongs to you and how God wants you to live right now:

1. You have a right to boldly approach the throne of God. You are God's child. You can go before the Father as His child, not like a beggar.

   "Therefore, having been justified by faith, we have peace with God through our Lord Jesus Christ, through whom also we have access by faith into this

grace in which we stand, and rejoice in hope of the glory of God." –Romans 5:1-2

"Let us therefore come boldly to the throne of grace, that we may obtain mercy and find grace to help in time of need." –Hebrews 4:16

2. You have the peace of God that surpasses all understanding, and the right to have joy and peace.

"And the peace of God, which surpasses all understanding, will guard your hearts and minds through Christ Jesus." –Philippians 4:7

"The Lord will give strength to His people; the Lord will bless His people with peace." –Psalm 29:11

3. You have the right to be healed and live a long life on the earth.

"No evil will conquer you; no plague will come near your home." –Psalm 91:10

"But He was wounded for our transgressions, He was bruised for our iniquities; The chastisement for our peace was upon Him, And by His stripes we are healed. –Isaiah 53:5

"Who Himself bore our sins in His own body on the tree, that we, having died to sins, might live for righteousness—by whose stripes you were healed." – 1 Peter 2:24

"With long life I will satisfy him, and show him My salvation." –Psalm 91:16

4. You have the right to prosper and have your needs met.

   "Do not fear, little flock, for it is your Father's good pleasure to give you the kingdom." –Luke 12:32

   "...let them say continually, "Let the Lord be magnified, who has pleasure in the prosperity of His servant." – Psalm 35:27

   "The thief does not come except to steal, and to kill, and to destroy. I have come that they may have life, and that they may have it more abundantly." – John 10:10

   "And my God shall supply all your need according to His riches in glory by Christ Jesus." – Philippians 4:19

   "And God is able to make all grace abound toward you, that you, always having all sufficiency in all things, may have an abundance for every good work." –2 Corinthians 9:8

   "He disarmed the spiritual rulers and authorities. He shamed them publicly by his victory over them on the cross." – Colossians 2:15

5. You have the right to be physically protected.

> "You are my hiding place; You shall preserve me from trouble; You shall surround me with songs of deliverance. Selah." – Psalm 32:7

> "But the Lord is faithful, who will establish you and guard you from the evil one." – 2 Thessalonians 3:3

> "No evil shall befall you, nor shall any plague come near your dwelling" –Psalm 91:10

6. You have the right to live free from fear.

> "I will not be afraid of ten thousands of people who have set themselves against me all around." –Psalm 3:6

> "Behold, God is my salvation, I will trust and not be afraid; For the Lord God is my strength and song, and He has become my salvation." –Isaiah 12:2

> In righteousness you shall be established; You shall be far from oppression, for you shall not fear; and from terror, for it shall not come near you. (Isaiah 54:14).

> "For you did not receive the spirit of bondage again to fear, but you received the Spirit of adoption by whom we cry out, "Abba, Father." –Romans 8:15

7. You have the right to live in a safe and secure dwelling.

> "My people will dwell in a peaceful habitation, In secure dwellings, and in quiet resting places." – Isaiah 32:18

He who dwells in the shelter of the Most High will abide in the shadow of the Almighty. I will say to the Lord, "My refuge and my fortress, my God, in whom I trust."
—Psalm 91:1-2

From the end of the earth I call to you when my heart is faint. Lead me to the rock that is higher than I, for you have been my refuge, a strong tower against the enemy. Let me dwell in your tent forever! Let me take refuge under the shelter of your wings! Selah – Psalm 61:2-4

8. You have a right to use the Name of Jesus.

   "And in that day you will ask Me nothing. Most assuredly, I say to you, whatever you ask the Father in My name He will give you." – John 16:23

   "And whatever you ask in My name, that I will do, that the Father may be glorified in the Son." –John 14:13

   "And these signs will follow those who believe: In My name they will cast out demons; they will speak with new tongues; they will take up serpents; and if they drink anything deadly, it will by no means hurt them; they will lay hands on the sick, and they will recover." – Mark 16:17-18

9. You have authority and power over the enemy in this world.

   "And they cast out many demons, and anointed with oil many who were sick, and healed them." –Mark 6:13

"And these signs will follow those who believe: In My name they will cast out demons; they will speak with new tongues; 18 they will take up serpents; and if they drink anything deadly, it will by no means hurt them; they will lay hands on the sick, and they will recover." – Mark 16:17-18

"Behold, I give you the authority to trample on serpents and scorpions, and over all the power of the enemy, and nothing shall by any means hurt you." –Luke 10:19

10. You have a right to expect good things in this life.

    "If you then, being evil, know how to give good gifts to your children, how much more will your Father who is in heaven give good things to those who ask Him!" – Matthew 7:11

11. You are greatly loved by God and clothed with compassion, kindness, humility, gentleness and patience.

    "Therefore, as the elect of God, holy and beloved, put on tender mercies, kindness, humility, meekness, longsuffering;" –Colossians 3:12

12. You are more than a conqueror through Him who loves you (Romans 8:37).

13. You have the Spirit of wisdom and revelation in the knowledge of Jesus, the eyes of your heart have been

enlightened, so that you know the hope of having life in Christ (Ephesians 1:17-18).

All these blessings and more are yours now, but God doesn't control whether you live them, you do. You must believe what God says.

Romans 10:17 tells us "Faith comes by hearing, and hearing by the word of God." So, the way to build or grow your faith is by:

- Hearing and reading the word of God out loud,
- Listening to the word of God being preached, taught, or recorded),
- Meditating and proclaiming the word of God.

As we do this, we renew our minds. As you renew your mind your thinking, and speaking will be transformed.

In Luke chapter 10 Jesus gives us the assurance that He has given us the power to overcome all the power of the enemy, and nothing shall harm us.

> *"[19] Behold, I give you the authority to trample on serpents and scorpions, and over all the power of the enemy, and nothing shall by any means hurt you. [20] Nevertheless do not rejoice in this, that the spirits are subject to you, but rather rejoice because your names are written in heaven." —Luke 10:19-20*

This authority is available through faith. Choose to believe what God says about you.

Practice Exercise #1:

Write down 3 or more things that God has done in your life to remind you that He is real, and He is a promise keeper:

_____

_____

_____

_____

_____

_____

_____

_____

_____

_____

Now write two or three prayer confessions based on your rights as a Believer for you or your loved ones:

Promises, Promises. God Always Keeps His Promises

Angeline L. Williams

Promise Maker, Promise Keeper

"The Lord shall increase you more and more, you and your children. Ye are blessed of the Lord which made heaven and earth." — *Psalm 115:14-15 (KJV)*

God's original intent for man was for us to be blessed, fruitful, multiply and have dominion (Genesis 1:28). He created humanity to be beings of increase. He is against any form of barrenness in your life—physical, mental, or spiritual. Barrenness has never been a part of God's plan for man. Lack and poverty entered the earth at the fall of in the Garden (Genesis 3:16-24). Victorious abundant living isn't just for heaven. Broke, sick, busted and disgusted brings no glory to God. It is still God's will that you and your descendants increase in every area of life while on earth (John 10:10). God wants you prosperous, and healthy!

God is a promise maker and a promise keeper. He always keeps His promises. With all the promises in the word of God, God has not promised that we will never have trouble. Believers get diseases and die just as non-believers. Believers have physical, emotional, and financial struggles just as non-believers.

One of my favorite lessons in scripture is when Jesus calms the storms. There are two instances where he does this. One was when Jesus was in the boat asleep and a Great Storm arose and the other was when He sent them into the storm.

> "35 On the same day, when evening had come, He said to them, "Let us cross over to the other side." 36 Now when they had left the multitude, they took Him along in the boat as He was. And other little boats were also with Him. 37 And a great windstorm arose, and the waves beat into the boat, so that it was already filling. 38 But He was in the stern, asleep on a pillow. And they awoke Him and said to Him, "Teacher, do You not care that we are perishing?"
>
> 39 Then He arose and rebuked the wind, and said to the sea, "Peace, be still!" And the wind ceased and there was a great calm. 40 But He said to them, "Why are you so fearful? How is it that you have no faith?" 41 And they feared exceedingly, and said to one another, "Who can this be, that even the wind and the sea obey Him!" — Mark 4:35-41 (NIV)

And in Mark chapter 6 it reads,

"⁴⁵ Immediately He made His disciples get into the boat and go before Him to the other side, to Bethsaida, while He sent the multitude away. ⁴⁶ And when He had sent them away, He departed to the mountain to pray. ⁴⁷ Now when evening came, the boat was in the middle of the sea; and He was alone on the land. ⁴⁸ Then He saw them straining at rowing, for the wind was against them. Now about the fourth watch of the night He came to them, walking on the sea, and would have passed them by. ⁴⁹ And when they saw Him walking on the sea, they supposed it was a ghost, and cried out; ⁵⁰ for they all saw Him and were troubled. But immediately He talked with them and said to them, "Be of good cheer! It is I; do not be afraid." ⁵¹ Then He went up into the boat to them, and the wind ceased. And they were greatly amazed in themselves beyond measure, and marveled. ⁵² For they had not understood about the loaves, because their heart was hardened." —Mark 6:45-52*

Notice that in both these instances Jesus spoke words. There is a great comparison here between the sea and life. Some days there is smooth sailing and because the nature of the sea is to produce storms, some days storms will arise. Whether Jesus is in your ship or not, you will have storms. If you are a nonbeliever, you are going to have storms. If are a follower of Christ, you are going to have storms. I don't think there's a person alive who has never been in a storm of some sort. God causes His sun to rise on the evil and the good, and sends rain on the righteous and the unrighteous (Matthew 5:45). This would lead some to believe that Believers are no better off than people in the world.

The Bible says Job was a holy man, yet he suffered, but just as God brought Job out of his affliction, He will bring us out too. If God allows it, He has a purpose. Think about it—sunshine and rain are both blessings to the world, and they both come from God, and they do not come by chance. If God allows it, He has a purpose.

Despite life's storms, the word of God assures us that He always keeps His promises, and He answers prayer. In Isaiah 46:11 God says,

> "From the east I summon a bird of prey; from a far-off land, a man to fulfill my purpose. What I have said, that I will bring about; what I have planned, that I will do."

Scripture assures us,

> "God is not a man, that He should lie, nor a son of man, that He should repent. Has He said, and will He not do? Or has He spoken, and will He not make it good?" — Numbers 23:19

> "My covenant I will not break, Nor alter the word that has gone out of My lips." —Psalm 89:34

Isaiah 30:18 tell us,

> *"For this reason the Lord is ready to show you mercy; he sits on his throne, ready to have compassion on you. Indeed, the Lord is a just God; all who wait for him in faith will be blessed." (NET)*

If you are one who sought God regarding certain things, and you feel as if God did not answer your prayer, or He did not answer as you expected. I want you to know that God does indeed answer the prayers of His children. Believe His Word.

> *"14 This is the confidence we have in approaching God: that if we ask anything according to his will, he hears us. 15 And if we know that he hears us—whatever we ask—we know that we have what we asked of him." —1 John 5:14-15 (NIV)*

> *"Ask and it will be given to you; seek and you will find; knock and the door will be opened to you." — Matthew 7:7 (NIV)*

> *"Before they call I will answer; while they are still speaking I will hear." —Isaiah 65:24*

If you haven't received the answer take an honest assessment of your life. Spend time with God in prayer to determine if a hindrance is blocking answers. There may be a few reasons why you haven't seen the answer:

- It may not be time yet; God is still working to make it happen. Have you heard the saying, "He's an on-time God. He may not come when you want Him to, but He's always on time? I know this to be true. Remember with the Lord a day is like a thousand years, and a thousand years are like a day. (2 Peter 3:8) Whether you are talking about now or twenty years from now, it's right now to God.
- Your motive may have been not according to the will of God (James 4:3),
- He may say as He said to Paul, *"My grace is sufficient for you, for my power is made perfect in weakness"* (2 Corinthians 12:7-9)

God says we are destroyed for lack of knowledge. Many of our problems are solved by getting God's wisdom, applying it, and trusting God with the rest. No matter what is going on realize, understand, believe that God wants to fulfill His promises for our lives. God does hear the Believer's prayers and God answers our prayers. Our experiences are never wasted. God will use the circumstances in our lives to grow us spiritually.

To see the fulfillment of God's promises in our life we must believe that the promises are for us and then confess what we believe.

> *"Let us hold fast the confession of our hope without wavering, for He who promised is faithful"* —Hebrews 10:23

It is easy to talk about what you believe. Telemarketing was a job that I would get to supplement my income as a single parent. I really didn't like doing this type of work, but a part-time position was easy to obtain. One thing I noticed was that if I didn't believe in the service or the product, I couldn't freely talk about it and convince anyone of the benefits because I wasn't convinced myself. We confess what we believe. If we don't believe the promises belong to us, how then can we confess them? We need to actively hold on to the promises of God, and declare them by faith.

It is through faith and patience that we receive the promises of God. Until the promise you are believing God for manifests, you will need to exercise patience and keep your eyes on Him.

There are several examples of this in the Bible:

- God promised that He won't destroy the world with flood again (Genesis 9:11). That promise is still standing today. While there are floods, there has not been a flood of the magnitude of the one that came before this promise.
- God promised Abraham a son through his wife Sarah even though both of them had well passed

childbearing age (Genesis 17:16). Abraham chose to believe God (Romans 4:16-21). Abraham waited for 25 years, from the time God made the promise until the promise was fulfilled. Abraham was 100 years old his son Isaac was born.

- God promised King David that he will always have a son on the throne of Judah. *"Your house and your kingdom will endure forever before me; your throne will be established forever" (2 Samuel 7:16).* In time, God fulfill this promise through his Son, Jesus.

- When Solomon became the king, he asked for wisdom. The Bible says that God gave Solomon a "breadth of understanding as measureless as the sand on the seashore."

- Through dreams, God promised Joseph that he would rise to a position of leadership over his parents and brothers. Joseph was seventeen years old when his brothers sold him into slavery. He was thirty when his final release from captivity came. (Genesis 37:2, 5-11, 41:1-46).

- All the promises God made to the Israelites through Moses were fulfilled. *"Praise be to the Lord, who has given rest to his people Israel just as he promised. Not one word has failed of all the good promises he gave through his servant Moses."* — *1 Kings 8:56*

- God sent the angel Gabriel to the virgin Mary to tell her that she would conceive and give birth to a son (Luke 1:26-31). God also promised Jesus' earthly father Joseph that Jesus would save His people from their sins (Matthew 1:21). Because God fulfills His promises, we have a Savior today!

These stories remind us that God always keeps His promises. Sometimes it may even seem that things are going in the opposite direction of what God has promised but hold on, if God said it, He will do it.

Praying God's word is an effective spiritual warfare tactic. Praying the heart of God back to Him for our family, friends and ourselves is very powerful. Since I've learned to use scripture as a model for my prayers, my faith has increased, I have drawn closer to God and come to understand His word more.

2nd Timothy 3:16 tells us,

"all scripture is inspired by God and profitable for teaching, for reproof, for correction and for training in righteousness."

The Greek word for 'inspired' is *theopneustos*, which means, God-breathed. The writers of Bible were selected by God as His instruments and assisted by the Spirit to record scripture. Even the people who translated the original scriptures from Hebrew and Greek were chosen by God and assisted by the Spirit.

2 Peter 1:21 says,

"for prophecy never came by the will of man, but holy men of God spoke as they were moved by the Holy Spirit."

1. Hebrews 4:12 says,

"For the word of God is living and powerful, and sharper than any two-edged sword, piercing even to the division of soul and spirit, and of joints and marrow, and is a discerner of the thoughts and intents of the heart."

God's Word reveals the good and the bad, the wise and the unwise. It is the primary tool in learning how to live the best possible life, free from the restraints of stumbling in darkness. It is also a powerful defensive weapon to protect us from the lies of the enemy. It is also a powerful defensive weapon to protect us from the lies of the enemy.

John 8:44 says Satan is the father of lies. Everything he whispers in our ear is a lie that is meant to steal, kill, and destroy. When we know the truth, we can use it to stand against his lies. Jesus prayed, *"Sanctify them by Your truth. Your word is truth"* (John 17:17).

Jesus demonstrated for us how to use scripture against Satan's lies in Luke 4:1-13. Each time Satan tempted Jesus, He responded with the truth of scripture. God's goal is to transform you—to help you become more like Christ. It will take practice, but your goal should be to respond like Jesus at any moment. Verse 13 says Satan departed for a season, indicating that he was coming back.

Remember what Ephesians 4:26-27 says,

"26 "Be angry, and do not sin": do not let the sun go down on your wrath, 27 nor give place to the devil."

When problems arise, when we face battles, when we experience spiritual warfare, the word of God is a light to our path. Our Father is faithful, He has us covered. He has never been defeated, and He has never lost a battle, and He never will. We are protected by the One who holds the universe in place (Psalm 95:3-5), backed by legions of angelic forces who come to our aid when we but whisper the name of Jesus in desperate need of help. Evil may appear to be prospering, but evil can only go so far because God has established its boundaries. We have nothing to fear. If God is for you, doesn't matter who is against you, they can't win. So, lift your head up high. The battle is not yours; it is the Lord's.

When we are born again, there are things we must learn, and unlearn, and habits we must break. Changing how you think, speak, and act is not an overnight process, and no matter how hard you try, it cannot be done without the Holy Spirit's help. Like babies, we will crawl, stumble, fall and struggle as we learn how to walk this new life. We must allow the Holy Spirit to come upon us and help us.

Galatians 5:22-23 says,

"22 But the fruit of the Spirit is love, joy, peace, long-suffering, kindness, goodness, faithfulness, 23 gentleness, self-control. Against such there is no law."

The Passion Translation says it like this:

"22-23 But the fruit produced by the Holy Spirit within you is divine love in all its varied expressions: joy that overflows, peace that subdues, patience that endures, kindness in action, a life full of virtue, faith that prevails, gentleness of heart, and strength of spirit. Never set the law above these qualities, for they are meant to be limitless."

This passage gives us the attributes that will be produced in our life by the Holy Spirit. When we open our hearts and allow the Lord to have His way within us, He begins to change us from the inside out. It will take some time, but if you make spending time in the word of God, speaking and praying God's word a priority your outlook will change and so will your circumstances.

God wants us to become skillful in the use of the Sword of the Spirit. In Ephesians chapter 6 Paul tells us to put on the Armor of God, which God has provided us for protection and to give us victory.

> "*¹¹ Clothe yourselves with the full armor of God, so that you will be able to stand against the schemes of the devil. ¹² For our struggle is not against flesh and blood, but against the rulers, against the powers, against the world rulers of this darkness, against the spiritual forces of evil in the heavens.*
>
> *¹³ For this reason, take up the full armor of God so that you may be able to stand your ground on the evil day, and having done everything, to stand. ¹⁴ Stand firm therefore, by fastening the belt of truth around your waist, by putting on the breastplate of righteousness, ¹⁵ by fitting your feet with the preparation that comes from the good news of peace, ¹⁶ and in all of this, by taking up the shield of faith with which you can extinguish all the flaming arrows of the evil one.*
>
> *¹⁷ And take the helmet of salvation and the sword of the Spirit (which is the word of God). ¹⁸ With every prayer and petition, pray at all times in the Spirit, and to this end be alert, with all perseverance and petitions for all the saints."* — *Ephesians 6:11-18 NET*

God provides this armor along with prayer, to help us stand triumphant in our spiritual battles. The Belt of Truth, the Breastplate of Righteousness, Shoes of the Gospel of Peace, the Shield of Faith, and the Helmet of Salvation serve as defense weapons in the armor of God. The sword of the Spirit is the offensive weapon in our armor.

One day during prayer, God spoke to me and said, "You battle with My word." As I began to study on the power of the word and apply it to my life, I could see and understand what God meant. God was saying that I needed to declare His word in the midst of what was going on and He would do the rest. Since Jesus defeated Satan and his evil spirits on the Cross, we can confidently put on the full armor of God and stand firm in Christ's victory for us.

The Bible says,

> *"For the word of God is living and powerful, and sharper than any two-edged sword, piercing even to the division of soul and spirit, and of joints and marrow, and is a discerner of the thoughts and intents of the heart." —Hebrews 4:12*

On one side the Word of God protects us and on the other side, it cuts down our enemy. We fight knowing that Jesus has already won the victory for us. We must know the Word of God and remain close to Him and His Word to do effectively use it against the devil. Jesus is the Vine, and we are the branches. A healthy and vibrant connection with Jesus producing fruit in our lives.

Meditating, studying, and memorizing the Word is important. As we do these things, our knowledge of the scriptures will increase. The word will become embedded in our hearts, and it will come out of us to fight the temptations of Satan, as it did with Jesus in the wilderness.

Keep in mind that prayer is simply communicating with our Heavenly Father. He knows our hearts, and He hears our desires, even when we can't say what we're feeling. As I said earlier, there is no specific way to pray. In fact, sometimes we can't pray. Scripture says if this happens, the Spirit will pray for us with groanings that can't be uttered. There are times all I can do is pray "Jesus, Jesus, Jesus" or "The Blood of Jesus" and that's enough. Then again praying the scriptures is a way I've found that helps me build my faith, and pray more specifically. I can't stress enough the importance of praying God's word.

Angeline L. Williams

Activating the Promises

> *"For those of us who believe, faith activates the promise, and we experience the realm of confident rest! For he has said, "I was grieved with them and made a solemn oath, 'They will never enter into the calming rest of my Spirit.'" God's works have all been completed from the foundation of the world, for it says in the Scriptures, and on the seventh day God rested from all his works." —Hebrews 4:3-4 The Passion Translation*

Why do some Believers experience an abundance of God's promises while some experience very little? I can't answer that question with a surety because I'm not in everyone's life, and every circumstance is different. However, I can say that the way we receive the rest of God's promises is the same way we received salvation, by faith. It is through faith alone that we possess the promises of God. So, let's talk about faith.

God does nothing in the earth apart from faith. He says in Hebrews 11:6 *"without faith it is impossible to please Him: for he that cometh to God must believe that He is, and that He is a rewarder of them that diligently seek Him."* Faith releases the power of God's word in our life. Faith is needed to access every promise of God including salvation.

Hebrews 11:1 in the Amplified Bible says,

> *"Now faith is the assurance (title deed, confirmation) of things hoped for (divinely guaranteed), and the evidence of things not seen [the conviction of their reality—faith comprehends as fact what cannot be experienced by the physical senses]."*

Now faith is the assurance, the confirmation, the title deed. Title deed means you own it. Say you are buying a house, well even though you are paying the mortgage every month, on time the house doesn't truly belong to you until you make that last mortgage payment, and you get the title deed. The promises of God belong to you. Jesus made the final payment on the Cross and transferred to you what rightfully belongs to you.

God gave you the faith—the title deed, so you can possess what belongs to you. Joshua became the leader of the Israelites after the death of Moses. God told Joshua to go and take the land that He had already given them. When you know what belongs to you, you go get it.

Most people think faith is another word for belief, or positive thinking. They think if they believe something is so, it will be. They try to believe so they can have what they want. When my daughter was diagnosed with a rare form of breast cancer, we both believed God that she would be healed. We even had similar dreams the same night of her healing. Then God showed us both that He was bringing her home to Heaven.

After she left, people said things to me like, "God promised us 70 years on earth, and we didn't believe hard enough; she just gave up; she stopped believing; she didn't have enough faith" and other thing along that line. How silly is it to think that a mere human is powerful enough to override God's will, plan, or purpose?

Hebrews 11:1 tells us that *"faith is the substance of things hoped for, the evidence of things not seen."* One translation says, *"faith is the assurance of things hoped for, the conviction of things not seen."* Question is, where does the substance, the evidence and the assurance come from? How do we get the conviction to believe? Is it something we develop within ourselves? Can we just muster up faith when want to?

Scripture tells us that Jesus is the author and finisher of our faith (Hebrews 12:2). God gives every person a measure of faith, no matter if they are born again or not.

> *"For I say, through the grace given to me, to everyone who is among you, not to think of himself more highly than he ought to think, but to think soberly, as God*

has dealt to each one a measure of faith." —Romans 12:3

So, faith is not something we can generate on our own. God loves us, and He knows that without faith it is impossible to please Him, He gives a measure of faith to everyone. (Hebrews 11:6) Faith is the method or tool that God uses to bring salvation to His people and deliver us from sin's consequences.

God wants people to first use this gift of faith to repent of their sin and accept Jesus Christ as Lord. Many people think that when they believe in Jesus that they somehow made faith appear, I used to think this way myself. However, God saves us by His grace through the faith He gives us.

Ephesians 2:8-9 says,

"8 For by grace you have been saved through faith, and that not of yourselves; it is the gift of God, 9 not of works, lest anyone should boast."

The scripture says faith is a gift from God, but many people think this scripture is saying because of our faith, grace enabled us to believe for salvation. If we could somehow believe in Jesus on our own, then salvation would be based on what we have done, not on what Jesus did. That would not be salvation but self-righteousness.

God's grace (unmerited favor) gives us the faith that enables us to believe Jesus Christ for salvation. Jesus said, "No one can come to Me unless the Father who sent Me draws him; and I will raise him up at the last day" (John 6:44). Although the Father's desire for all to be saved, sadly, some will not use the faith gives them for salvation.

So now let's look at how powerful this faith is that God gives us. As Believers we are to walk by faith, not by sight. We live by the faith (2 Corinthians 5:7, Romans 1:17).

Paul said in Galatians 2:20,

"I am crucified with Christ: nevertheless, I live; yet not I, but Christ liveth in me: and the life which I now live in the flesh I live by the faith of the Son of God, who loved me, and gave himself for me."

Some translations have changed the words to say, "faith in," rather than faith of but the Apostle Paul does not refer to faith in Christ, but the faith of Christ. Paul understood that Christ was in him, that he no longer lived according to the old man or old way of thinking. The life he now lived was by the faith of the Son of God.

Peter and John understood this truth. One day they were on their way to the temple for prayer. They came upon a crippled man begging alms. Look at what was said.

"And his name—by faith in his name—has made this man strong whom you see and know, and the faith

that is through Jesus has given the man this perfect health in the presence of you all." —Acts 3:16

Peter and John knew the man was healed by the faith of Jesus. Many Believers fast and pray asking God for faith, more faith, or great faith. Many people hope and pray to get to the place where they no longer live, but that Christ would live in them. We have the same faith that Paul, Peter and John had. Jesus lives in us therefore we have the same faith Jesus has.

So, the faith of the Son of God helps us to completely trusts in the power of God and His word. Faith and confession go hand in hand. Confession is speaking and testifying what we believe in our hearts. It is affirming something that we believe and witnessing for a truth that we have embraced.

The psalmist said in Psalm 116:10 *"I believed; therefore, I spoke."* The Apostle Paul in 2 Corinthians 4:13 wrote, *"Since we have the same spirit of faith...we also believe and therefore speak."* Confessing the word of God without faith in God and His word is just spouting words out of your mouth. But when you confess God's word in faith, you are agreeing with and saying what God says.

Jesus said that we can have what we say if we believe what we say.

> "*²⁰ As they passed by in the morning, they saw the fig tree withered away to its roots. ²¹ And Peter remembered and said to him, "Rabbi, look! The fig tree that you cursed has withered." ²² And Jesus answered them, "Have faith in God. ²³ Truly, I say to you, whoever says to this mountain, 'Be taken up and thrown into the sea,' and does not doubt in his heart, but believes that what he says will come to pass, it will be done for him. ²⁴ Therefore I tell you, whatever you ask in prayer, believe that you have received it, and it will be yours." —Mark 11:20-24 ESV*

Jesus said we can speak to the things that hinder us,

> "*²² So Jesus answered and said to them, "Have faith in God. ²³ For assuredly, I say to you, whoever says to this mountain, 'Be removed and be cast into the sea,' and does not doubt in his heart, but believes that those things he says will be done, he will have whatever he says." —Mark 11:22-23*

Jesus told the disciples that with faith in God (or the God kind of faith), if they believed and spoke to the problem, issue or whatever it is they could experience the same results He did.

When you pray and confess God's Word, things happen in the spirit realm. Things get aligned, and realigned according to God's will and purpose. Many times, God uses His angels to set things up for us. God's angels are ministering spirits sent forth to serve those who will inherit salvation (Hebrews 1:14). In the Bible we God's angels as guardians, warriors, messengers and ministering spirits, waiting on God's people.

Psalm 103:20-21 says,

"20 Bless the Lord, you His angels, who excel in strength, who do His word, heeding the voice of His word. 21 Bless the Lord, all you His hosts, You ministers of His, who do His pleasure."

The scripture says angels heed the voice of God's Word. The Bible does not actually have a voice unless we give it a voice. When we speak God's word in faith, we give it a voice. They are His Words, not ours so it as if He has spoken it Himself. The angels of God will react to that word the same way as if God were speaking it.

Most of us have learned over the years to speak and think contrary to what God speaks. Just as the angels of God wait on us to speak what God has declared so they can move on our behalf Satan and his demons are perched waiting for your doubt, unbelief, and conversation. Their job is to get you to say something that God did not say. Their goal is your destruction. He has been doing that since the Garden of Eden.

Look at what Psalm 39:1 in the Living Bible says,

> "I said to myself, I'm going to quit complaining! I'll keep quiet, especially when the ungodly are around me."

Listen, demons are around you 24/7 so be careful how you use your mouth. Jesus said in Luke 6:45 that whatever is in the heart overflows into speech. Therefore, we should continually put God's truth into our hearts so the kind of words we speak will be aligned with what God speaks. We do this by listening to, reading, studying, and meditating on God's word.

> "But what does it say? "The word is near you, in your mouth and in your heart" (that is, the word of faith which we preach): that if you confess with your mouth the Lord Jesus and believe in your heart that God has raised Him from the dead, you will be saved." —Romans 10:8-9

Jesus said to the disciples,

> "17 And these signs shall follow them that believe; In my name shall they cast out devils; they shall speak with new tongues; 18 They shall take up serpents; and if they drink any deadly thing, it shall not hurt them; they shall lay hands on the sick, and they shall recover." —Mark 16:17-18

Jesus promises to the disciples and us today that these things shall happen when we follow the ground rules:

- they must believe, and
- they must do the work,

The disciples went forth speaking the word and the Lord worked with them confirming the word spoken with signs following. (Mark 16:20). Many healings occurred, and multitudes believed on the Lord because the apostles believed and acted on the word spoken.

Your words must line up with the word of God if you want to activate His promises. Signs follow the Word of God. God moves in line with His Word. God stresses the importance of the words we speak throughout the Bible.

In Proverbs 18:7 He says,

"A fool's mouth is his destruction, and his lips are the snare of his soul."

In Proverbs 18:20-21 He says,

"A man's stomach is filled with the fruit of his mouth. With the harvest of his lips, he is satisfied. Death and life are in the power of the tongue; those who love it will eat its fruit."

Proverbs 21:23 says,

"Whoever guards his mouth and tongue keeps his soul from troubles."

James 3:6 in the Message translation says,

> "A careless or wrongly placed word out of your mouth can do that. By our speech we can ruin the world, turn harmony to chaos, throw mud on a reputation, send the whole world up in smoke and go up in smoke with it, smoke right from the pit of hell."

So, if we have been experiencing an abundance of negative things, we should check what we have been believing in our heart and confessing with our mouth. We should want our confession to be the same as God's. Confession can also be a way of calling things that be not as though they are. When God spoke the world into existence, He did not speak about what surrounded Him, He spoke what He wanted to see.

> "In the beginning God created the heaven and the earth. And the earth was without form, and void; and darkness was upon the face of the deep. And the Spirit of God moved upon the face of the waters. And God said, Let there be light: and there was light." —Genesis 1:1-3

The Israelites did not watch what they spoke. They constantly complained even after seeing God perform miracle after miracle for them, and they died in the wilderness at the door of the promise. Their children were set back forty years before they entered the Promised Land. When they entered the Promised Land the ten spies who brought back the bad report of the land, died by a plague before the

LORD. Your mouth can easily undo any blessing God wants you to receive.

I did not understand that many of the trials and struggles I was experiencing were because of my negative confessions. I blamed others thinking that they were wishing and speaking evil on me. I blamed the devil and I doubted God. While it is true that the devil is our adversary much of what I endured was because of what I was confessing. One day, as I was complaining yet again, God interrupted me and said, "Put My Word in your mouth."

Once God opened my understanding to the power of my words, I repented for how I had been speaking against the Grace that God had placed in my life, and for blocking His hand to bless me and my family.

Jesus said,

> "Truly I tell you, if anyone says to this mountain, 'Go, throw yourself into the sea,' and does not doubt in their heart but believes that what they say will happen, it will be done for them." —Mark 11:23

Through faith our mouth can move mountains, but often our mouth is moved by our mountains. You might notice that things get worse when this happens.

Proverbs 30:32 warns us,

"If thou hast done foolishly in lifting up thyself, or if thou hast thought evil, lay thine hand upon thy mouth."

If you have a negative thought the scripture says the next thing to do is cover your mouth. Why? To prevent you from speaking and giving it life to that thought, and speaking against the grace God has spoken over you.

God says in Isaiah 55:10-11,

"10 For as the rain cometh down, and the snow from heaven, and returneth not thither, but watereth the earth, and maketh it bring forth and bud, that it may give seed to the sower, and bread to the eater: 11 So shall my word be that goeth forth out of my mouth: it shall not return unto me void, but it shall accomplish that which I please, and it shall prosper in the thing whereto I sent it."

Hebrews 4:12 says the word of God is living and active. It is living and vibrant and carries the power of life and transformation. It is persistent and it keeps working until it accomplishes the purpose it is intended for. Scripture tells us God spoke, and the universe came into existence. He issued the decree, and it stood firm (Psalm 33:9). Nothing and no one can stop God's word from completing its mission.

Watch Out For Those Snares

It would be nice, but it is highly unlikely that living the victorious Christian life will be void of troubles.

> *"I have spoken to you, that in Me you may have peace. In the world you will have tribulation; but be of good cheer, I have overcome the world." —John 16:33*

I wasn't sure if I should approach the subject of spiritual warfare in this book. However, just like with the book Put the Word In Your Mouth, unbelievable warfare came up against me as I was writing, so I decided to at least touch on it. Although I shouldn't be, I'm still baffled by the warfare that came against me and who it came from. To me, the level of warfare indicates how afraid the enemy is for the Saints of God to receive the message of praying God's promises. There are several books on the subject of the power of the words we speak, but I believe because it is something that God really wants the Body of Christ to grasp, God is continually bringing the message before us.

There is a spiritual war daily in the spiritual realm led by Satan and his demonic spirits against God. Satan wants to be a god. He fights for the possession of the soul (mind, will, and emotions) of the Saints and he wants to dominate the unredeemed spirit of unsaved people. Most of the time spiritual warfare is external disguised as major life challenges, but we also face battles that are internal as well. Satan's tactics often involve exploiting our emotions, such as grief, disappointment, insecurity, shame, and loneliness. He tries to embarrass us, and discredit us and the weapons God has given us to fight the good fight of faith and live victoriously.

We are so accustomed to seeing life's struggles and problems in non-spiritual terms that we automatically seek non-spiritual solutions for our problems. And so, we end up in a cycle of the same issues over and over. While some will say not everything is related to spiritual warfare, the Bible tells us we have an enemy who is consistently out to destroy us.

The devil is diabolical and very subtle. On his war path Satan goes for the jugular vein in his assaults against the Believers. He especially goes after true ministers of Jesus Christ. He will harass, denigrate, and lie on them and use anything and everyone to distract and destroy us. Family members, other Christians, and others we are close to are the ones he uses the most. He knows that the power of life and death is in the power of the tongue. He wants you to get angry and speak harm on them rather than blessings. He wants you to sin with your mouth. He wants to use you to curse them. No matter how angry you get, don't do it!

John 10:10 says the thief (Satan) to steal, and to kill, and to destroy. If he can't destroy you right off, then he will distract you in an attempt to set you up for destruction. The Bible warns us of how fiendish Satan is yet, so many in the Body of Christ have not grasped the power of our words and are not aware of just how malicious and persistent Satan is. You must take this seriously. If we fall for Satan's traps, snares, and distractions then we become ineffective in our faith and our witness.

Remember what Ephesians 6:12 says,

"For we do not wrestle against flesh and blood, but against principalities, against powers, against the rulers of the darkness of this age, against spiritual hosts of wickedness in the heavenly places."

Recognize that it is the devil and his evil forces who is behind how the person is acting. I believe every trial that we go through and every unhealthy habit or emotion, whether it is anger, strife, bitterness, unforgiveness, pride, low self-esteem, insecurity, emotional instability, and more are connected to the war of good and evil that is waged daily in the spiritual world. Understand that this is not a fight that you can fight with your own strength or words. It is a spiritual fight, and it cannot be fought in the flesh. It is a fight that can only be fought in the spiritual realm, on your knees and with God's word.

We need to stay alert so we can recognize his traps, so we won't fall prey to the enemy. 1st Thessalonians 5:6 tells us let us not sleep, as others do, but let us watch and be sober. In 1st Peter 5:8 Peter compares Satan to a lion. Lions seek prey that displays signs of weakness.

Once he spots one who appears slow, tired, or weak, he sneaks around it, waiting for the perfect opportunity to attack. He then kills his victim by breaking its neck or suffocating it by clamping his jaws around its throat. When he comes across a herd, he will roar to create panic, then run after the herd seeking a slow, weak one, and then he moves in for the kill. Lions like to sneak around and hide. They don't want the prey to be aware of their presence.

This is exactly what Satan does to Believers. He sneaks around, disguised as an angel of light (2 Corinthians 11:14) creating situations to distract us, and when it seems we have fallen prey he attacks. He wants to suffocate us spiritually and shut our mouths or convince us to talk about the problem, complain, and stop us from praying.

It is also important for you to know and understand that Satan and demons are not omnipresent, omniscient, or omnipotent. Satan's strength, reach, and authority are limited and under the authority of our heavenly Father. Look what God says through His prophet Isaiah,

> *"14 In righteousness you shall be established; You shall be far from oppression, for you shall not fear; and*

from terror, for it shall not come near you. ¹⁵ *Indeed they shall surely assemble, but not because of Me. Whoever assembles against you shall fall for your sake.* ¹⁶ *"Behold, I have created the blacksmith Who blows the coals in the fire, Who brings forth an instrument for his work; and I have created the spoiler to destroy.* ¹⁷*No weapon formed against you shall prosper, and every tongue which rises against you in judgment you shall condemn. This is the heritage of the servants of the Lord, and their righteousness is from Me," says the Lord." —Isaiah 54:14-17*

My point is, if God allows it, He has a purpose that will benefit us and the Kingdom of God. So, seek God on what to do and say regarding every issue or trial you face. Ask, seek, and knock.

Prayer for Spiritual Attack:

Let us pray:

Heavenly Father I know this battle is not with flesh and blood, but against principalities, against powers, against the rulers of darkness of this age, against spiritual wickedness in high places, therefore, I ask for Your help to remember when attacks come to not get angry and sin but to stand boldly in the whole armor of God, that I may be able to withstand in the evil day, and having done all to stand.

I choose to think on the things that are true, honorable, right, pure, lovely, of good repute, of excellence and anything worthy of praise (Philippians 4:6-8). I choose to praise You in the midst of this attack for I know that if you are for me and Your plans for me are good.

It is written in Zephaniah 3:17, "The Lord your God is in your midst, a mighty one who will save; he will rejoice over you with gladness; he will quiet you by his love; he will exult over you with loud singing. So, I will stand strong in You Lord, and in the power of Your might according (Ephesians 6:10-13). For Christ the hope of glory is in me (Colossians 1:27). In Jesus' name I pray. Amen.

Pray After This Manner ...

Psalm 119:105 says that the Word of God is a lamp for our feet and a light for our path. In other words, the Word of God will shine light on our dark circumstances, and show us the way we should go to allow God's will to flow in our life. The Bible gives us instruction, wisdom, and truth because it is relevant to our lives.

Jesus taught us to pray,

> *"9 After this manner therefore pray ye: Our Father which art in heaven, Hallowed be thy name. 10 Thy kingdom come, Thy will be done in earth, as it is in heaven. 11 Give us this day our daily bread. 12 And forgive us our debts, as we forgive our debtors. 13 And lead us not into temptation, but deliver us from evil: For thine is the kingdom, and the power, and the glory, for ever. Amen."*

Prayer is our Heavenly Father's will. Praying for God's will to be done acknowledges that we accept what God is doing is over our desires. Praying using God's Holy Word is the most powerful thing we can do for ourselves and others.

As you pray God's Word for you and others, you are partnering with God for His will to be done on earth as it is in Heaven. As you pray in Jesus' name you join hands with Jesus, who constantly intercedes for us to our Heavenly Father.

Scripture tells us in James chapter five,

"The prayer of a righteous man is powerful and effective. Elijah was a man just like us. He prayed earnestly that it would not rain, and it did not rain on the land for three and a half years. Again, he prayed, and the heavens gave rain, and the earth produced its crops." —James 5:16-18

The Amplified Bible says: The earnest (heartfelt, continued) prayer of a righteous man makes tremendous power available [dynamic in its working].

It is the Believers, the Body of Christ who are the righteous. We have been made righteous through Christ (Romans 3:22). The KJV Dictionary defines effectual as, "producing an effect, or the effect desired or intended; or having adequate power or force to produce the effect.

The word fervent means impassioned, forceful, passionate, heartfelt, powerful, or wholehearted. James saying that a passionate, wholehearted prayer will accomplish much, implies that a half-hearted prayer will not be as effective.

The scripture says Elijah was a man just like you and me. How could Elijah make such a claim? What caused him to have such bold courage? Elijah had an intimate and close fellowship with God. He could sense God's burdens, purposes, and desires. This is what happens in close relationships. Elijah was convinced and confident in God and His word. The scripture does not say it, but I believe Elijah was led by The Spirit of God and spoke according to what God had already spoken.

> *"16 Make sure you do not turn away to serve and worship other gods! 17 Then the anger of the Lord will erupt against you, and he will close up the sky so that it does not rain. The land will not yield its produce, and you will soon be removed from the good land that the Lord is about to give you." —Deuteronomy 11:16-17 (NET)*

> *"23 The sky above your heads will be bronze and the earth beneath you iron. 24 The Lord will make the rain of your land powder and dust; it will come down on you from the sky until you are destroyed." —Deuteronomy 28:23-24 (NET)*

In 1st Kings 17:1 Elijah declared to King Ahab,

> *"As the Lord God of Israel lives, before whom I stand, there shall not be dew nor rain these years, except at my word."*

Again, God spoke what God said. God promised rain and Elijah believed Him. He knew that if God promised rain, the rain would surely come. So, when He spoke to the King and told him to eat and prepare for rain, he was confident that rain would come (1 Kings 18:1).

1st John 5:14–15 says,

"This is the confidence we have in approaching God: that if we ask anything according to his will, he hears us. And if we know that he hears us—whatever we ask—we know that we have what we asked of him."

Having an intimate relationship with God through the Scriptures and prayer will bring the type of courage that Elijah had. God's burdens, purposes, and desires will become priority and when you do this the blessings that already belong to you will just show up at the appointed time.

"But above all pursue his kingdom and righteousness, and all these things will be given to you as well." — *Matthew 6:33 (NET)*

Fervent prayer displays a passionate intensity. Effectual, fervent prayer can come from scripture or the depths of our own hearts however, when it comes from our heart it should line up or agree with the will of God, with what God has declared, with His already established word (Psalm 119:89). This type of prayer comes from an intimate relationship with God. We have all heard people say negative things about God's Word, but be like Paul and call those things dung. Take up God's word and believe it. Study and meditate on the letters to the church today, Acts to Jude. Read them, study them, and believe.

The Old Testament Prophets, our Savior Jesus Christ, and the people of the early church understood the power of praying in agreement with what God has already declared. Prayer was also a constant in their lives. I have seen God do some miraculous things through prayer and standing on His word. If you do not learn to put God's word in your mouth and pray and believe God, you will live defeated.

There are many benefits of praying God's Word back to Him. Praying God's word will help you focus and keep your prayers centered in God's will. When you pray God's word you are praying as a righteous child of God. When you pray righteously you pray with the confidence that whatever you pray God is going to hear you. How do you know that God heard you and that you have what you prayed for? You know because you prayed according to His will.

> "For the eyes of the Lord are on the righteous, and His ears are open to their prayers; but the face of the Lord is against those who do evil." —1 Peter 3:12

Keep in mind Satan does not want you to pray, which is why it is so easy to drift off and get distracted during prayer. Some of us pray lists of complaints, and even try to tell God how to handle things, and answer. Don't do that, stay focused. If you find yourself doing this writing out scripture-based prayers and praying the scriptures will help you stay focused.

Once you pray something, the fight begins. The devil comes almost immediately to plant doubt in your mind, bring thoughts of the issue and steal the word. So, if you think something that negates the prayer or the Rhema Word God spoke during prayer, put your hand over your mouth, don't speak those thoughts (Proverbs 30:32). Let praise come out of your mouth.

If you have something that you have not confessed before the Lord, then confess it. Especially if the Holy Spirit brings it into your mind. Confess it to God, repent and let it go. Then act like, talk like the child of God that you are.

> *"8 If we say that we have no sin, we deceive ourselves, and the truth is not in us. 9 If we confess our sins, He is faithful and just to forgive us our sins and to cleanse us from all unrighteousness. 10 If we say that we have not sinned, we make Him a liar, and His word is not in us." — 1 John 1:8-9*

God wants to bless you. He wants to use you, but He cannot use you guilty. Satan will constantly accuse you and bring guilt before you to make you feel as if you are unworthy to be blessed. So again, I say confess your faults to God and He will forgive you and cleanse you from all unrighteousness, then let it go.

Listen, when God suggests the impossible to you do not try to figure out how He's going to do it, or how is it's going to work, only believe.

> *"35 While He was still speaking, some came from the ruler of the synagogue's house who said, "Your daughter is dead. Why trouble the Teacher any further?" 36 As soon as Jesus heard the word that was spoken, He said to the ruler of the synagogue, "Do not be afraid; only believe."* — Mark 5:36

It may take some time for you to renew your mind to this principle and make this a habit, so if you speak against the prayer ask God to forgive you and pray again. Don't leave those negative words out there in the atmosphere for Satan to use against you.

When I first started praying scripture back to God, I did not realize how limited my prayers and my prayer life was. Since then, my prayer life has increased. It has helped me study God's word more, understand scriptures better and spend more time with Him.

God has a promise, and an answer in His word for everything we face. So, when I am faced with a situation, or when I don't know what to pray, I seek God on what scriptures to pray, or I search for scriptures according to my need. When I find the scriptures, I write them down and meditate on them. Then I develop a prayer and confession from them, write them down and pray them until I sense a breakthrough. This way I know I am agreeing with, praying God's will, and pray confidently. This is how I came up with the prayers and confessions included in this book and in the book *Put The Word In Your Mouth*.

The more you do this, the more you are planting it in your heart. The Word becomes a part of you and will naturally spring up from inside you when you need it. Your thoughts begin to turn to worshipping God and thanksgiving, confession, and prayers for yourself and others. I have seen many miracles because of prayer and speaking the promise rather than the problem, including being healed of cancer and experienced other miracles.

Please understand when we pray, stand on and confess God's promises we cannot have the attitude of holding the promises over God's head to get what we want. We cannot manipulate God and we don't need to try for Psalm 37:4 tells us, Delight yourself also in the Lord, and He shall give you the desires of your heart.

Keys To Answered Prayer

First, decide what you want from and, and find the scripture that promises you that. Don't let your what you want or what you are believing God for be limited by what other people say.

Then pray and believe you have what you ask for. Mark 11:24 says,

"Therefore I tell you, whatever you ask for in prayer, believe that you have received it, and it will be yours."

2 Corinthians 1:20 NIV tells us,

"For no matter how many promises God has made, they are "Yes" in Christ. And so through him the "Amen" is spoken by us to the glory of God."

Do you see that? The "Amen" (the agreement, the so be it) is spoken by us. Listen, if you find it in Bible, it is your promise. Say Amen to it.

One more thing. When did God make the promise? Was it when you asked for it or was it before the foundation of the world, before your mother and father ever thought of you? He made the promise before the foundation of the world. God dwells outside of time. He is not limited by time because there is no time with God. Faith, which is of God, is also outside of time. It is higher than time. The promise and the answer to your prayer was prepared and sent before the foundation of the world. So, whether you're talking about today or 10 years from now, it's right now to God. Believe you received when you pray. Because we have been living by an internal clock, it is hard for the mind to grasp this truth.

Faith dictates to time, what time it is. As humans we see things through an internal clock or physical time. Because of Christ we can now look beyond the veil, which has been ripped and destroyed (Mark 15:37–38). The separation between God and humanity, between man and man, and even between woman and man was destroyed. This is a scripture word that you can stand on for your family. So now, for you to get a different view, move outside of time. We can now see in the spiritual realm through our spiritual eyes. The Father will help you do this if you ask (2 Kings 6:17-20).

Believing is a choice. You must choose to believe. Say with me,

> *"I choose to believe God, even when it looks impossible, even though no one has ever done it, I choose to believe God because I'm connected to God and I am in line with God's promise all things have been made possible for me because I have a God, a Father who makes all things possible! If He said it, I believe it!"*

Finally, let every thought confirm you have what you asked God for. As I've said, this is where the battle really begins. This is where you will have to fight the good fight of faith.

The Bible says in Philippians 4:6-8,

"⁶ Do not be anxious about anything, but in every situation, by prayer and petition, with thanksgiving, present your requests to God. ⁷ And the peace of God, which transcends all understanding, will guard your hearts and your minds in Christ Jesus. ⁸ Finally, brothers and sisters, whatever is true, whatever is noble, whatever is right, whatever is pure, whatever is lovely, whatever is admirable—if anything is excellent or praiseworthy—think about such things."

In other words, manage your mind. Don't rehearse the problem in your mind or through your mouth. Say what God says. The more you say it, the more you believe it. The more you believe it, the more you say it. The more you say it, the more you believe it. The more you believe it, the more you say it. Before long you will be like fully persuaded that what God promised He is well able to perform it.

The power of prayer is not dependent on whether we are a pastor, or leader in the church or how long we have been a member of a church. It doesn't matter whether we pray whether standing, sitting or kneeling.

1st John 5:14–15 says,

> *"This is the confidence we have in approaching God: that if we ask anything according to his will, he hears us. And if we know that he hears us—whatever we ask—we know that we have what we asked of him."*

Our righteousness in Christ, faith in God, and His Word is what makes our prayers powerful. For our prayers to be effective, they must be in agreement with the will of God. Effectual, fervent prayer can come from scripture or from the depths of our own hearts. As we grow the two become intertwined.

When we pray the Word of God in faith at least two things happen:

1. We are confessing that we believe and trust in God's and His Word.
2. We are releasing His word into the atmosphere, so it can accomplish things according to God's purpose. Remember, God said that His Word will not return to Him void (incomplete, unfulfilled) but it will accomplish what He pleases, and it will prosper wherever He sends it.

Have you ever practiced sitting quietly before God with no distractions except your thoughts? In a world full of hustle and bustle this can seem to be really be hard to do. It takes practice, but it is a practice with great reward. Your prayer time should include sitting quietly before God often. King David actually spoke to his soul and told it to wait:

> "⁵ My soul, wait silently for God alone, for my expectation is from Him. ⁶ He only is my rock and my salvation; He is my defense; I shall not be moved. ⁷ In God is my salvation and my glory; The rock of my strength, and my refuge, is in God. ⁸ Trust in Him at all times, you people; Pour out your heart before Him; God is a refuge for us. Selah." —Psalm 62:5-8

Find a quiet time and a quiet place where you feel comfortable.

> "But you, when you pray, go into your room, and when you have shut your door, pray to your Father who is in the secret place; and your Father who sees in secret will reward you openly." —Matthew 6:6

As Christians we're filled with the Holy Spirit and have God's Spirit with us 24/7. We are God's children, but remember even when praying His promises, we can't dictate to God what He should do. But we can come boldly, and respectfully before His throne with an attitude of humility and expectancy.

Ask the Lord what He wants you to pray. He's got something to say to you so listen for God's voice. Pay attention to where you feel encouraged, passionate, or stirred to take action. Talk to God about what you're reading in the Bible when you pray. Treat it like a conversation.

You can also use a concordance or do a search online to find Bible passages that address issues that are your heart. When you select relevant scriptures meditate on them. You can use the scriptures here in the book as well. Let God open up the passage to you to get the understanding God wants you to get.

Read the scriptures out loud, meditating on each word and verse. As we read and pray God's Word out loud our faith grows. Faith comes by hearing (Romans 10:17). Reflect on what the passage is saying to you today. The thing about scripture is you can read a passage and a new revelation can come just about each time.

Keep a prayer journal. Write down the scriptures and what so you can come back to them repeatedly. It will help you memorize scripture as well as see how faithful God is in answering your prayers. Personalize the scriptures to fit your situation by inserting "I" or "me," your name or the names of people you are praying for. I type mine up and print them out and tape them to the wall and pray them over and over.

Practice Exercise #2:

You can pray any part of the Bible. Also, from Genesis to Revelation, you will find prayers that you can pray. The books of Psalm and Isaiah are a couple of my favorite choices which includes promises and prayers. So, let's do a little practice exercise. Read the following passages of scripture and write out a prayer for you or your loved ones:

Psalm 40:

_____

_____

_____

_____

_____

_____

_____

_____

_____

_____

Psalm 34:

Promises, Promises. God Always Keeps His Promises

Psalm 121:

Promises, Promises. God Always Keeps His Promises

Psalm 116:

Angeline L. Williams

Psalm 23:

Promises, Promises. God Always Keeps His Promises

Psalm 91:

Angeline L. Williams

Stand on God's Promises

> *Grace and peace be multiplied to you in the knowledge of God and of Jesus our Lord, as His divine power has given to us all things that pertain to life and godliness, through the knowledge of Him who called us by glory and virtue, by which have been given to us exceedingly great and precious promises, that through these you may be partakers of the divine nature, having escaped the corruption that is in the world through lust." —2 Peter 1:2-4*

We have all had promises made to us that went unfulfilled. We've made some promises with good intentions to fulfill them, but despite our best effort we could not make them happen. The truth is, we all fall short or fail to perform every promise made. God has given us His promises, and in His promises, He has given us everything we will ever need for this life and our eternal life. A promise is a written oral or agreement to do or not to do something; a vow, a declaration or assurance that someone will do a particular thing, or a particular thing will happen; a basis for expectation. People make all kinds of promises, sometimes without realizing how others may interpret them. Legally if a person makes a statement or a promise that causes another party to rely on that statement, then the courts will enforce the promise as if it was a completed contract.

It's been my experience that God is the only One who can make a promise and then fulfill it without fail. That is one truth I remind myself of when things seem to be going haywire in my life. God cannot lie. His Word is settled (Psalm 119:89). God cannot and will not go contrary to His Word.

A requirement of a legally binding document is that is put in writing and signed by the parties concerned. In the Bible God has put promises in writing to help us when we call on Him, to provide for us, to empower us, to protect and deliver us when we are in trouble, to give us peace and so many other promises.

King Solomon trusted God's promises. In his temple dedication prayer he said,

> *"Praise be to the Lord, who has given rest to his people Israel just as he promised. Not one word has failed of all the good promises he gave through his servant Moses." —1 Kings 8:56*

Standing on the unconditional promise that God does not change like people do gives me hope (Numbers 23:19). Remembering this helps me trust that God will do just as He and His word says. When we are standing on the promises of God, we cannot fail because the promises of God cannot fail. Standing on the promises of God gives me boldness in prayer.

Again, I encourage you don't give up if the promise is not manifested right away.

Paul says in Hebrews 6:13,

"When God made his promise to Abraham, since there was no one greater for him to swear by, he swore by himself."

2nd Corinthians 1:20 tells us that all the promises of god in Him are Yes, and in Him Amen, to the glory of God through us.

The Living Bible says it like this,

"He [talking about Jesus] carries out and fulfills all of God's promises, no matter how many of them there are; and we have told everyone how faithful he is, giving glory to his name."

Another promise that brings me hope is 1 John 1:9 which says,

"If we confess our sins, he is faithful and just and will forgive us our sins and purify us from all unrighteousness."

It is comforting to know that once we ask God to forgive us, He does and then forgets about it (Micah 7:19, Isaiah 1:18, Psalm 103:12). When we put our faith and trust in Christ for salvation and confess our sins God completely takes away our guilt.

> *"I acknowledge my sin unto thee, and mine iniquity have I not hid. I said, I will confess my transgressions unto the Lord; and thou forgavest the iniquity of my sin. Selah."* —Psalm 32:5

I want to talk about this for a bit because some people believe because our sins are forgiven past, present, and future that the consequences of their sinful choices are erased.

Paul said in Galatians 6:7, "Do not be deceived: God is not mocked, for whatever one sows, that will he also reap." This does not change our redemption. We are forgiven! However, it is important to understand that there is a difference between forgiveness of sin and the consequences of sin. While it is true that our sins are forgiven past, present, and future, we still need to confess our sins, and we still may have to pay the consequences of our sin because sin leads to negative consequences.

For example, the thief dying with Jesus on the Cross was completely forgiven, yet he was still crucified (Luke 23:39-43). His sins were erased in God's sight, but he still suffered the punishment for his crime. David was a man after God's own heart, yet he committed adultery, and then he sent the woman's husband into battle to be murdered. Needless to say, God was not pleased. David repented and turned back to God, yet David had to face the consequences of his actions. David had a son that was conceived through his adulterous affair who died, and David faced tremendous turmoil within his family.

God can forgive a person who commits adultery or fornication who confesses his sin and repents, but if the person they commit the sin with has an STD they can get the disease even though they are saved. If we don't take care of the body we have been given, we may be forgiven, but our health may suffer, and we may never fully recover.

So even when we receive forgiveness, the effects of our sin can remain while living in this fallen world. Don't let this discourage you, because despite the circumstance God is with you! When we draw near to the Lord during such consequences, God can use those negative consequences in many ways for our spiritual growth.

God is a promise keeping God. He promised in Isaiah 54:10,

> "For the mountains shall depart and the hills be removed, but My kindness shall not depart from you, nor shall My covenant of peace be removed."

In Psalm 89:34 God says,

"My covenant I will not break, nor alter the word that has gone out of My lips."

God always keeps His promises. He does not promise something and then remove it because we displease Him. If you are going through a challenging situation right now, or you've experienced a difficult or tragic event, I encourage you to build your faith upon God's promises, not upon your experiences.

Scripture Promises

"Man shall not live by bread alone but by every word that proceeds out of the mouth of God." — Matthew 4:4

In the following sections I have gathered scripture promises that you can meditate on and pray. These promises are rightfully yours as a child of God. Accept them. Believe them. Act upon them. Take God at his word.

Psalm 66:18 says if we regard iniquity in our heart, the Lord will not hear so, if there is hatred, bitterness, jealousy, lust, unforgiveness, or anything the Holy Spirit brings to mind, repent and ask the Lord for His forgiveness. Forgive anyone you need to forgive.

Do your part of the promise, then trust God to do His part. If the promise says pray, then pray. If it says believe, then you believe and expect God to act. After you have done these things, praise God for the answer. Look at God's word like medicine. Declare the promises as many times a day as necessary while you wait on the Lord's answer.

Remember God will keep His promise.

Guidance and Help

Psalm 139:16 says of God, *"Your eyes have seen my formless substance; and in Your book were written all the days that were ordained for me, When as yet there was not one of them."* (NASB)

God knows the way we should go because He has ordained it before the foundation of the world (Jeremiah 29:11). He orders the steps of the righteous (Psalm 37:23). Therefore, He freely gives His wisdom and guidance to anyone who seeks Him. He desires to give us His wisdom and guidance, but He will not force us to listen to Him. However, our life will be better if we choose to yield to His direction and His purpose for my life. The only thing that can keep us from the Lord's guidance is an unyielding spirit. We must keep our eye on God, and decree the promise, not the problem.

Here are some promises on God's guidance and help. Some are commands, and some are promises. Meditate on these passages. Ask the Holy Spirit to help you understand the ones that stand out to you. Use these scriptures and others that come to mind and write down a couple of prayer confessions in the lesson in this section declaring your faith in God to answer your prayer. Keep in mind that no promises or scripture will help you if you don't put it into action.

Promises, Promises. God Always Keeps His Promises

If the passage is a command do what it says. Don't worry about it, pray about it. God always keeps His promises.

Proverbs 3:6: In all your ways acknowledge Him, and He shall direct your paths.

Psalm 23:3: He restoreth my soul: He leadeth me in the paths of righteousness for His Name's sake.

Psalm 37:4: Though he may stumble, he will not fall, for the Lord upholds him with his hand.

Psalm 48:14: For this God is our God for ever and ever; he will be our guide even to the end.

Psalm 31:3: For Thou art my Rock and my Fortress; therefore for Thy Name's sake lead me, and guide me.

Psalm 32:8: I will instruct thee and teach thee in the way which thou shalt go: I will guide thee with mine eye.

Psalm 33:11: The counsel of the Lord stands forever, The plans of His heart from generation to generation.

Isaiah 41:13: For I am the Lord your God who takes hold of your right hand and says to you, Do not fear; I will help you.

Isaiah 30:21: Whether you turn to the right or to the left, your ears will hear a voice behind you, saying, "This is the way; walk in it."

Isaiah 42:16: And I will bring the blind by a way that they knew not; I will lead them in paths that they have not known: I will make darkness light before them, and crooked things straight. These things will I do unto them, and not forsake them.

Psalm 48:14: For this is God, our God forever and ever; He will be our guide even to death.

Isaiah 58:11: The Lord will guide you always; he will satisfy your needs in a sun-scorched land and will strengthen your frame. You will be like a well-watered garden, like a spring whose waters never fail.

Hebrews 6:17-18: [17] Thus God, determining to show more abundantly to the heirs of promise the immutability of His counsel, confirmed it by an oath, [18] that by two immutable things, in which it is impossible for God to lie, we might have strong consolation, who have fled for refuge to lay hold of the hope set before us.

Genesis 28:15: I am with you and will watch over you wherever you go, and I will bring you back to this land. I will not leave you until I have done what I have promised you.

John 10:3-4: The gatekeeper opens the gate for him, and the sheep listen to his voice. He calls his own sheep by name and leads them out. When he has brought out all his own, he goes on ahead of them, and his sheep follow him because they know his voice.

John 16:13: Howbeit when He, the Spirit of Truth, is come, He will guide you into all Truth: for He shall not speak of Himself; but whatsoever He shall hear, that shall He speak: and He will show you things to come.

Practice Exercise #3:

_____

_____

_____

_____

_____

_____

_____

_____

_____

_____

Angeline L. Williams

God's Goodness

All of us experience challenging times, some more than others. Sometimes we bring difficulty on ourselves, and sometimes things happen that we have no control over. When things get tough, it's easy to focus on us and the difficulties before us, however, doing this will only lead to more problems. No matter where you find yourself today knowing, believing, and receiving the goodness of God will help you get through.

Here are some of my favorite scriptures about God's goodness. When problems try to disturb your peace meditate on them, and others that come to mind and write down a couple of prayer confessions in the lesson in this section declaring your faith in God to lead you and give you wisdom. Don't worry about it, pray about it. God always keeps His promises.

Exodus 34:6: And the Lord passed by before him, and proclaimed, The Lord, The Lord God, merciful and gracious, longsuffering, and abundant in goodness and truth. (KJV)

Psalm 86:5: For You, Lord, are good, and ready to forgive, and abundant in mercy to all those who call upon You.

Psalm 103:13-14: As a father pities his children, so the Lord pities those who fear Him. For He knows our frame; He remembers that we are dust.

Psalm 23:6: Surely goodness and mercy shall follow me all the days of my life; and I will dwell in the house of the Lord forever.

James 1:17: Every good gift and every perfect gift is from above, and comes down from the Father of lights, with whom there is no variation or shadow of turning.

Matthew 7:11: If you then, being evil, know how to give good gifts to your children, how much more will your Father who is in heaven give good things to those who ask Him!

Practice Exercise #4:

_____

_____

_____

_____

Promises, Promises. God Always Keeps His Promises

Angeline L. Williams

For Healing

Here are some promises on Healing. Some are commands, and some are promises. Meditate on these passages. Ask the Holy Spirit to help you understand the ones that stand out to you. Use these scriptures and others that come to mind and write down a couple of prayer confessions in the lesson in this section declaring your faith in God to answer your prayer. Don't worry about it, pray about it. God always keeps His promises.

Exodus 15:26: I will put none of the diseases on you which I have put on the Egyptians; for I, the LORD, am your healer.

Psalm 41:3: The Lord will sustain, refresh, and strengthen him on his bed of languishing; all his bed You [O Lord] will turn, change, and transform in his illness. (AMP)

Psalm 91:16: "With a long life I will satisfy him And let him see My salvation."

Psalms 103:3: Who pardons all your iniquities, who heals all your diseases.

Psalms 107:20: He sent His word and healed them, and delivered them from their destructions.

Psalm 118:17: I shall not die, but live, and declare the works of the Lord.

Proverbs 18:21: Death and life are in the power of the tongue, and those who love it will eat its fruit.

Isaiah 40:31: But those who wait for the Lord [who expect, look for, and hope in Him] shall change and renew their strength and power; they shall lift their wings and mount up [close to God] as eagles [mount up to the sun]; they shall run and not be weary, they shall walk and not faint or become tired. (AMP)

Isaiah 41:10: Fear not [there is nothing to fear], for I am with you; do not look around you in terror and be dismayed, for I am your God. I will strengthen and harden you to difficulties, yes, I will help you; yes, I will hold you up and retain you with My [victorious] right hand of rightness and justice. (AMP)

Isaiah 53:5: But He was pierced through for our transgressions, He was crushed for our iniquities; The chastening for our well-being fell upon Him, and by His scourging we are healed.

Jeremiah 17:14: Heal me, O LORD, and I will be healed; save me and I will be saved, for You are my praise.

Jeremiah 30:17: For I will restore you to health and I will heal you of your wounds, declares the LORD.

Proverbs 4:20-22: My son, give attention to my words; incline your ear to my sayings. Do not let them depart from your sight; keep them in the midst of your heart. For they are life to those who find them and health to all their body.

Matthew 8:8: But the centurion said, 'Lord, I am not worthy for You to come under my roof, but just say the word, and my servant will be healed.'

Matthew 9:35: Jesus was going through all the cities and villages, teaching in their synagogues and proclaiming the gospel of the kingdom, and healing every kind of disease and every kind of sickness.

Luke 6:19: And all the people were trying to touch Him, for power was coming from Him and healing them all.

Galatians 3:13: Christ has redeemed us from the curse of the law, having become a curse for us (for it is written, "Cursed is everyone who hangs on a tree."

Hebrews 13:8: Jesus Christ is the same yesterday and today and forever.

James 5:14-15: Is anyone among you sick? Then he must call for the elders of the church and they are to pray over him, anointing him with oil in the name of the Lord;

and the prayer offered in faith will restore the one who is sick, and the Lord will raise him up...

3 John 1:2: Beloved, I pray that in all respects you may prosper and be in good health, just as your soul prospers.

1 Peter 2:24: And He Himself bore our sins in His body on the cross, so that we might die to sin and live to righteousness; for by His wounds you were healed.

2 Corinthians 12:9: And he said unto me, My grace is sufficient for thee: for my strength is made perfect in weakness. Most gladly therefore will I rather glory in my infirmities, that the power of Christ may rest upon me.

Philippians 2:27: For indeed he was sick nigh unto death: but God had mercy on him; and not on him only, but on me also, lest I should have sorrow upon sorrow.

Romans 8:11: But if the Spirit of Him who raised Jesus from the dead dwells in you, He who raised Christ from the dead will also give life to your mortal bodies through His Spirit who dwells in you.

Practice Exercise #5:

Angeline L. Williams

Protection

Here are some promises on God's protection. Some are commands, and some are promises. Meditate on these passages. Ask the Holy Spirit to help you understand the ones that stand out to you. Use these scriptures and others that come to mind and write down a couple of prayer confessions in the lesson in this section declaring your faith in God for protection. If the passage is a command do what it says. Don't worry about it, pray about it. God always keeps His promises.

Deuteronomy 33:12: The beloved of the LORD dwells in safety. The High God surrounds him all day long, and dwells between his shoulders.

Deuteronomy 31:6: Be strong and courageous. Do not be afraid or terrified because of them, for the Lord your God goes with you; he will never leave you nor forsake you.

Hebrews 13:6: So we say with confidence, "The Lord is my helper; I will not be afraid. What can mere mortals do to me?"

Job 11:18-19: You will feel secure, because there is hope; you will look around and take your rest in security.

You will lie down, and none will make you afraid; many will court your favor.

Psalms 9:9: The LORD is a stronghold for the oppressed, a stronghold in times of trouble.

Psalms 27:5: For in the time of trouble He shall hide me in His pavilion; In the secret place of His tabernacle He shall hide me; He shall set me high upon a rock.

Psalms 54:4: Behold, God is my helper; the Lord is the upholder of my life.

Psalms 91:9-11: Because you have made the LORD your dwelling place – the Most High, who is my refuge – no evil shall be allowed to befall you, no plague come near your tent. For he will command his angels concerning you to guard you in all your ways.

Psalms 121:7-8: The LORD will keep you from all evil; he will keep your life. The LORD will keep your going out and your coming in from this time forth and forevermore.

Psalm 125:2: As the mountains surround Jerusalem, so the LORD surrounds his people, from this time forth and forevermore.

Proverbs 18:10: The name of the LORD is a strong tower; the righteous man runs into it and is safe.

Isaiah 46:3-4: "Listen to Me, O house of Jacob, and all the remnant of the house of Israel, who have been upheld by Me from birth, who have been carried from the womb: even to your old age, I am He, and even to gray hairs I will carry you! I have made, and I will bear; even I will carry, and will deliver you.

Isaiah 54:17: No weapon forged against you will prevail, and you will refute every tongue that accuses you. This is the heritage of the servants of the Lord, and this is their vindication from me," declares the Lord.

Practice Exercise #6:

_____

_____

_____

_____

_____

_____

_____

_____

Angeline L. Williams

For Prayer

We all need help with things in life, even with prayer. When we pray our minds can wonder, and sometimes, especially when we are overcome with emotion or faced with a crisis, we may find it hard to know how to pray, our prayer can become self-centered. Also, for some of us it's difficult to relinquish control, and we even attempt to tell God how to answer and meet our needs.

We don't know half the things we think we know. We need the wisdom of God. Paul says in Romans 8:26 that the Holy Spirit helps us pray the way we should. This is why I am an advocate of inviting the Holy Spirit to help you pray. This is why I am an advocate of praying scriptures.

Here are some promises for help with prayer. Some are commands, and some are promises. Meditate on these passages. Ask the Holy Spirit to help you understand the ones that stand out to you. Use these scriptures and others that come to mind and write down a couple of prayer confessions in the lesson in this section declaring your faith in God to answer your prayer. Keep in mind that no promise or scripture will help you if you don't put it into action. If the passage is a command do what it says. Don't worry about it, pray about it. God always keeps His promises.

Psalm 37:4-5: Delight yourself also in the Lord, and He shall give you the desires of your heart. Commit your way to the Lord, trust also in Him, and He shall bring it to pass.

Psalm 145:18-19: The Lord is near to all who call upon Him, to all who call upon Him in truth. He will fulfill the desire of those who fear Him; He also will hear their cry and save them.

Psalm 91:1-4: He who dwells in the shelter of the Most High will abide in the shadow of the Almighty. I will say to the Lord, "My refuge and my fortress, my God, in whom I trust." For he will deliver you from the snare of the fowler and from the deadly pestilence. He will cover you with his pinions, and under his wings you will find refuge; his faithfulness is a shield and buckler.

Isaiah 65:24: And it shall come to pass, that before they call, I will answer; and while they are yet speaking, I will hear.

Jeremiah 33:3: Call unto me, and I will answer you, and show you great and mighty things, which you know not.

Zephaniah 3:9: For then I will restore to the peoples a pure language, that they all may call on the name of the Lord, to serve Him with one accord.

2 Chronicles 7:14: If my people, which are called by my name, shall humble themselves, and pray, and seek my face, and turn from their wicked ways; then will I hear from heaven, and will forgive their sin, and will heal their land. (KJV)

Matthew 7:8: For everyone who asks receives, and he who seeks finds, and to him who knocks it will be opened.

Matthew 18:18-19: Assuredly, I say to you, whatever you bind on earth will be bound in heaven, and whatever you loose on earth will be loosed in heaven. "Again I say to you that if two of you agree on earth concerning anything that they ask, it will be done for them by My Father in heaven."

Matthew 21:33: And all things, whatsoever you shall ask in prayer, believing, you shall receive.

John 15:7: If you abide in me, and my words abide in you, ask whatever you wish, and it will be done for you.

Romans 8:26-27: Likewise the Spirit also helps in our weaknesses. For we do not know what we should pray for as we ought, but the Spirit Himself makes intercession for us with groanings which cannot be uttered. Now He who searches the hearts knows what the mind of the Spirit is, because He makes intercession for the saints according to the will of God.

James 1:5: If any of you lacks wisdom, let him ask God, who gives generously to all without reproach, and it will be given him.

James 5:14-16: Is anyone among you sick? Let him call for the elders of the church, and let them pray over him, anointing him with oil in the name of the Lord. And the prayer of faith will save the sick, and the Lord will raise him up. And if he has committed sins, he will be forgiven. Confess your trespasses to one another, and pray for one another, that you may be healed. The effective, fervent prayer of a righteous man avails much.

John 14:13-14: And whatever you ask in My name, that I will do, that the Father may be glorified in the Son. If you ask anything in My name, I will do it.

John 16:23-24: And in that day you will ask Me nothing. Most assuredly, I say to you, whatever you ask the Father in My name He will give you. Until now you have asked nothing in My name. Ask, and you will receive, that your joy may be full.

Galatians 4:6: And because you are sons, God has sent forth the Spirit of His Son into your hearts, crying out, "Abba, Father!"

1 John 5:14-15: Now this is the confidence that we have in Him, that if we ask anything according to His will, He hears us. 15 And if we know that He hears us, whatever we ask, we know that we have the petitions that we have asked of Him.

Practice Exercise #7:

Angeline L. Williams

Strength And Power

In this uncertain world, strength and courage are vital to our Christian walk. Here are some verses that strengthen and encourage me. Some are commands, and some are promises. Meditate on these passages. Ask the Holy Spirit to help you understand the ones that stand out to you. Use these scriptures and others that come to mind and write down a couple of prayer confessions in the lesson in this section declaring your faith in God for the strength and power you need to keep moving forward. Keep in mind that no promise or scripture will help you if you don't put it into action. If the passage is a command do what it says. Don't worry about it, pray about it. God always keeps His promises.

Exodus 15:2: The Lord is my strength and my song; he has given me victory. This is my God, and I will praise him—my father's God, and I will exalt him!

Deuteronomy 31:8 It is the Lord who goes before you. He will be with you; he will not fail you or forsake you. Do not fear or be dismayed.

2 Chronicles 16:9: For the eyes of the LORD run to and fro throughout the whole earth, to give strong support to those whose heart is blameless toward him.

Psalm 29:11: The Lord will give strength unto his people; the Lord will bless his people with peace.

Psalm 31:24: Be strong and confident, all you who wait on the LORD!

Psalm 32:7-8: You are my hiding place; you will protect me from trouble and surround me with songs of deliverance.

Psalm 34:17: When the righteous cry for help, the Lord hears, and rescues them from all their troubles.

Psalm 46:1-3: God is our refuge and strength, an ever-present help in trouble. Therefore we will not fear, though the earth give way and the mountains fall into the heart of the sea, though its waters roar and foam and the mountains quake with their surging.

Psalms 55:22: Cast your burden on the LORD, and he will sustain you; he will never permit the righteous to be moved.

Psalms 68:35: Awesome is God from his sanctuary; the God of Israel – he is the one who gives power and strength to his people. Blessed be God!

Psalm 73:26: My flesh and my heart may fail, but God is the strength of my heart and my portion forever.

Psalm 94:14-15: Certainly the LORD does not forsake his people; he does not abandon the nation that belongs to him. For justice will prevail, and all the morally upright will be vindicated.

Psalms 118:14: The LORD is my strength and my song; he has become my salvation.

Proverbs 18:10: The name of the Lord is a strong tower; the righteous run into it and are safe.

Nehemiah 8:10: Do not grieve, for the joy of the Lord is your strength.

Isaiah 40:29: He gives strength to the weary and increases the power of the weak.

Isaiah 40:31: But those who hope in the Lord will renew their strength. They will soar on wings like eagles; they will run and not grow weary; they will walk and not be faint.

Isaiah 41:10: So do not fear, for I am with you; do not be dismayed, for I am your God. I will strengthen you and help you; I will uphold you with my righteous right hand.

Isaiah 54:4: Do not be afraid; you will not be put to shame. Do not fear disgrace; you will not be humiliated. You will forget the shame of your youth and remember no more the reproach of your widowhood.

Jeremiah 31:25: For I will satisfy the weary soul, and every languishing soul I will replenish.

Zephaniah 3:17: The LORD your God is in your midst; he is a warrior who can deliver. He takes great delight in you; he renews you by his love; he shouts for joy over you.

Zechariah 4:6: Not by might, nor by power, but by my Spirit, says the LORD of hosts.

Zechariah 10:12: I will make them strong in the LORD, and they shall walk in his name, declares the LORD.

1 Chronicles 16:11: Seek the LORD and his strength; seek his presence continually!

2 Timothy 1:7: For God did not give us a Spirit of fear but of power and love and self-control.

Ephesians 6:10: Finally, be strong in the Lord and in his mighty power.

Prayer Confession for Strength And Power

Halleluiah! Father I thank You that I am born of God and have the strength to overcome the evil one and all manner of sin and temptation. For greater is he

(Jesus Christ) who dwells within me, than the enemy that is in the world. Eternal God You are my refuge. Under Your everlasting arms I can rest. Your eyes run to and fro throughout the whole earth, to give strong support to those who belong to You.

You did not give me a Spirit of fear but of power and love and self-control. You said, "I will make them strong in the LORD, and they shall walk in his name, declares the LORD." Therefore I stand strong in the Lord and in his mighty power. For You are in my midst to deliver and renews me by Your love. Thank You Father. In Jesus' name. Amen.

(1 John 4:4, Deuteronomy 33:27, 2 Chronicles 16:9, 2 Timothy 1:7, Zechariah 10:12, Ephesians 6:10, Zephaniah 3:17)

Practice Exercise #8:

_____

_____

_____

_____

_____

Angeline L. Williams

Promises, Promises. God Always Keeps His Promises

For Provision

Believing God for provision in the midst of a financial storm can be hard. It is even harder when you don't know how long the difficulty will last. Our Heavenly Father promises to meet the spiritual, emotional, and physical needs of all of His children.

Here are some promises for provision. Some are commands, and some are promises. Meditate on these passages. Ask the Holy Spirit to help you understand the ones that stand out to you. Use these scriptures and others that come to mind and write down a couple of prayer confessions in the lesson in this section declaring your faith in God for provision. Keep in mind that no promise or scripture will help you if you don't put it into action. If the passage is a command do what it says. Don't worry about it, pray about it. God always keeps His promises.

Genesis 8:22: While the earth remains, seedtime and harvest, and cold and heat, and summer and winter, and day and night shall not cease.

Deuteronomy 8:18: But you shall remember the LORD your God, for it is He who is giving you power to make wealth, that He may confirm His covenant which He swore to your fathers, as it is this day.

Deuteronomy 28:6: You will be blessed when you come in and blessed when you go out.

Deuteronomy 28:11-12: And the Lord shall make thee plenteous in goods, in the fruit of thy body, and in the fruit of thy cattle, and in the fruit of thy ground, in the land which the Lord swore unto thy fathers to give thee. The Lord shall open unto thee his good treasure, the heaven to give the rain unto thy land in his season, and to bless all the work of thine hand: and thou shalt lend unto many nations, and thou shalt not borrow.

Psalms 23:1-2: The LORD is my shepherd; I shall not want. He maketh me to lie down in green pastures: he leadeth me beside the still waters.

Psalm 34:9-10: Oh, fear the Lord, you His saints! There is no want to those who fear Him. The young lions lack and suffer hunger; But those who seek the Lord shall not lack any good thing.

Psalm 81:10: "I, the Lord, am your God, Who brought you up from the land of Egypt; Open your mouth wide and I will fill it. *(For Believer today Egypt represents the land of bondage, our old life of slavery to sin.)*

Psalms 84:11: For the LORD God is a sun and shield: the LORD will give grace and glory: no good thing will he withhold from them that walk uprightly.

Proverbs 3:9-10: ⁹ Honor the Lord with your possessions, and with the firstfruits of all your increase; ¹⁰ So your barns will be filled with plenty, and your vats will overflow with new wine.

Isaiah 65:24: Before they call I will answer; while they are yet speaking I will hear (ESV).

Malachi 3:10: Bring the whole tithe into the storehouse, so that there may be food in My house, and test Me now in this," says the Lord of hosts, "if I will not open for you the windows of heaven and pour out for you a blessing until it overflows.

Matthew 6:25-26: Therefore I say to you, do not worry about your life, what you will eat or what you will drink; nor about your body, what you will put on. Is not life more than food and the body more than clothing? Look at the birds of the air, for they neither sow nor reap nor gather into barns; yet your heavenly Father feeds them. Are you not of more value than they?

Matthew 11:28: "Come to Me, all who are weary and heavy-laden, and I will give you rest.

Matthew 7:7: Ask, and it will be given to you; seek, and you will find; knock, and it will be opened to you.

Matthew 7:11: If you then, who are evil, know how to give good gifts to your children, how much more will your

Father who is in heaven give good things to those who ask him!

John 14:13-14: Whatever you ask in my name, this I will do, that the Father may be glorified in the Son. If you ask me anything in my name, I will do it.

John 15:7: If you abide in me, and my words abide in you, ask whatever you wish, and it will be done for you.

John 15:16: You did not choose me, but I chose you and appointed you that you should go and bear fruit and that your fruit should abide, so that whatever you ask the Father in my name, he may give it to you.

John 16:23-24: In that day you will ask nothing of me. Truly, truly, I say to you, whatever you ask of the Father in my name, he will give it to you. Until now you have asked nothing in my name. Ask, and you will receive, that your joy may be full.

Romans 8:32: He who did not spare his own Son but gave him up for us all, how will he not also with him graciously give us all things?

Philippians 4:19: But my God shall supply all your need according to his riches in glory by Christ Jesus.

2 Corinthians 9:8: And God is able to make all grace abound toward you, that you, always having all sufficiency in all things, may have an abundance for every good work.

1 John 3:22: And whatever we ask we receive from him, because we keep his commandments and do what pleases him.

Prayer for Provision

Father God, You are the Creator of all things. You are worthy to receive glory and honor and power, for it is only because of You that the universe, the earth, and all of its inhabitants exist. The earth and everything in it belong to You. You promised that if I am willing and obedient, I will eat the best from the land, that I will not only continue to eat and be provided for, but I will eat the best from the land. I desire to always be willing and obedient to You, Father forgive me for times when I have been unwilling and disobedient. I choose to honor You with my life, my substance and the firstfruits of all you give me. I choose to seek You and Your kingdom first, to trust You and to obey You. You have promised that as I do, You will open the floodgates of heaven and pouring blessings I do not have enough room for it all. I proclaim I live in the overflow of blessings. I declare that every resource You have given me to produce income will overflow.

Father, You are my Provider. Thank You for restoring what was held up and stolen from me. Thank You for generously providing all that I need. In Jesus' name I pray. Amen.

(Revelation 4:11, Matthew 7:7, Psalm 24:1, Isaiah 1:19, Matthew 6:33, Proverbs 3:9-10, Malachi 3:10, Joel 2:25, 2 Corinthians 9:8)

Practice Exercise #9:

_____

_____

_____

_____

_____

_____

_____

_____

_____

Angeline L. Williams

For Times of Doubt

Here are some Bible scriptures and promises for when you begin to doubt. Some are commands, and some are promises. Meditate on these passages. Ask the Holy Spirit to help you understand the ones that stand out to you. Use these scriptures and others that come to mind and write down a couple of prayer confessions in the lesson in this section declaring your faith in God to answer your prayer. Keep in mind that no promise or scripture will help you if you don't put it into action. If the passage is a command do what it says. Don't worry about it, pray about it. God always keeps His promises.

Psalm 23: The Lord is my shepherd; I shall not be in want. He makes me lie down in green pastures, he leads me beside quiet waters, he restores my soul. He guides me in paths of righteousness for his name's sake. Even though I walk through the valley of the shadow of death, I will fear no evil, for you are with me; your rod and your staff, they comfort me. You prepare a table before me in the presence of my enemies. You anoint my head with oil; my cup overflows. Surely goodness and love will follow me all the days of my life, and I will dwell in the house of the Lord forever.

Psalm 34:15: The eyes of the Lord are on the righteous and his ears are attentive to their cry.

Isaiah 55:10-11: "For as the rain comes down, and the snow from heaven, and do not return there, but water the earth, and make it bring forth and bud, that it may give seed to the sower and bread to the eater, so shall My word be that goes forth from My mouth; It shall not return to Me void, but it shall accomplish what I please, and it shall prosper in the thing for which I sent it.

Isaiah 59:1: Behold, the LORD'S hand is not so short that it cannot save; nor is His ear so dull that it cannot hear.

Mark 11:22-23: Have faith in God. Truly I say to you, whoever says to this mountain, Be taken up and cast into the sea, and does not doubt in his heart, but believe that what he says is going to happen, it will be granted him.

Mark 11:24: Therefore I say to you, all things for which you pray and ask, believe that you have received them, and they will be granted you.

Luke 12:29-31: And do not seek what you will eat and what you will drink, and do not keep worrying. For all these things the nations of the world eagerly seek; but your Father knows that you need these things. But seek His kingdom, and these things will be added to you.

Romans 4:20-21: Yet, with respect to the promise of God, he did not waver in unbelief but grew strong in faith, giving glory to God, and being fully assured that what God had promised, He was able also to perform. When you lie down, you will not be afraid; When you lie down, your sleep will be sweet.

Matthew 7: 7-8: Ask and it will be given to you; seek and you will find' knock and the door will be opened to you. For everyone who asks receives he who seeks finds; and to him who knocks, the door will be opened.

Matthew 7:9-11: Which of you, if his son asks for bread, will give him a stone? Or if he asks for a fish, will give him a snake? If you, then, though you are evil, know how to give good gifts to your children, how much more will your Father in heaven give good gifts to those who ask him!

Philippians 4:13: I can do all things through Christ who strengthens me.

2 Timothy 1:7: For God has not given us a spirit of fear, but of power and of love and of a sound mind.

James 5:16: The effective prayer of a righteous man can accomplish much.

Romans 10:17: So faith comes from hearing, and hearing by the word of Christ.

1 Thessalonians 5:24: Faithful is He who calls you, and He also will bring it to pass.

Angeline L. Williams

Practice Exercise #10:

Promises, Promises. God Always Keeps His Promises

For Impatience

Are you impatient waiting for things to happen? Here are some of my favorite scriptures to help you to wait on the Lord. Some are commands, and some are promises. Meditate on these passages. Ask the Holy Spirit to help you understand the ones that stand out to you. Use these scriptures and others that come to mind and write down a couple of prayer confessions in the lesson in this section declaring your faith in God to settle you, and surround you with love. Keep in mind that no promise or scripture will help you if you don't put it into action. If the passage is a command do what it says. Don't worry about it, pray about it. God always keeps His promises.

Psalm 37:7-9: Rest in the Lord; wait patiently for him to act...

Psalm 40:1: I waited patiently for the Lord; he inclined to me and heard my cry.

Isaiah 25:9: And it shall be said in that day, Lo, this is our God; we have waited for him, we will be glad and rejoice in his salvation.

Isaiah 40:31: They that wait upon the Lord shall renew their strength; they shall mount up with wings as eagles;

they shall run, and not be weary; and they shall walk, and not faint.

Ecclesiastes 3:1: There is an appointed time for everything. And there is a time for every event under heaven. (NASB)

Lamentations 3:25-27: The Lord is good to those who wait for him, to the soul who seeks him. It is good that one should wait quietly for the salvation of the Lord. It is good for a man that he bear the yoke in his youth.

Galatians 6:9: And let us not grow weary while doing good, for in due season we shall reap if we do not lose heart.

Ephesians 4:2: I therefore, a prisoner for the Lord, urge you to walk in a manner worthy of the calling to which you have been called, with all humility and gentleness, with patience, bearing with one another in love.

Philippians 4:6: Do not be anxious about anything, but in everything by prayer and supplication with thanksgiving let your requests be made known to God.

James 1:12: Blessed is a man who perseveres under trial; for once he has been approved, he will receive the crown of life, which the Lord has promised to those who love him. (NASB)

Practice Exercise #11:

Promises, Promises. God Always Keeps His Promises

For Times Of Persecution

Are you facing times of persecution for things to happen. Here are some of my favorite scriptures to help you trust the Lord. Some are commands, and some are promises. Meditate on these passages. Ask the Holy Spirit to help you understand the ones that stand out to you. Use these scriptures and others that come to mind and write down a couple of prayer confessions in the lesson in this section declaring your faith in God to settle you, and surround you with love. Keep in mind that no promise or scripture will help you if you don't put it into action. If the passage is a command do what it says. Don't worry about it, pray about it. God always keeps His promises.

Deuteronomy 20:4: For the Lord your God is the one who goes with you, to fight for you against your enemies, to save you.

Proverbs 25:21-22: If your enemy is hungry, give him bread to eat; and if he is thirsty, give him water to drink; for so you will heap coals of fire on his head, and the Lord will reward you. The Lord your God fights for you, just as he has promised.

Psalm 5:11: But let all those rejoice who put their trust in You; let them ever shout for joy, because You defend them; Let those also who love Your name be joyful in You.

Psalm 55:22: Give your burdens to the Lord. He will carry them. He will not permit the godly to slip or fall.

Psalm 103:6: The Lord executes righteousness and justice for all who are oppressed.

Psalm 146:8: The Lord opens the eyes of the blind; the Lord raises those who are bowed down; the Lord loves the righteous.

1 Samuel 2:9: He will keep the feet of his saints, and the wicked shall be silent in darkness; for by strength shall no man prevail.

Zephaniah 3:17: The Lord your God is in your midst, a victorious warrior. He will exult over you with joy, he will be quiet in his love, he will rejoice over you with shouts of joy.

Matthew 5:10: Blessed are those who are persecuted for righteousness' sake, for theirs is the kingdom of heaven.

Matthew 5:44-45: Love your enemies! Pray for those who persecute you! In that way you will be acting as true sons of your father in heaven.

2 Timothy 2:12: If we endure, we shall also reign with Him. If we deny Him, He also will deny us.

1 Peter 4:14: If you are reproached for the name of Christ, blessed are you, for the Spirit of glory and of God rests upon you. On their part He is blasphemed, but on your part He is glorified.

Practice Exercise #12:

_____

_____

_____

_____

_____

_____

_____

_____

_____

_____

_____

Promises, Promises. God Always Keeps His Promises

For Times Of Grief

I know how tough periods of grief can be to get through. Here are some Bible scriptures and promises for when grief comes. Some are commands, and some are promises. Meditate on these passages. Ask the Holy Spirit to help you understand the ones that stand out to you. Use these scriptures and others that come to mind and write down a couple of prayer confessions in the lesson in this section declaring your faith in God to answer your prayer. Keep in mind that no promise or scripture will help you if you don't put it into action. If the passage is a command do what it says. Don't worry about it, pray about it. God always keeps His promises.

Psalm 23:4: Yea, though I walk through the valley of the shadow of death, I will fear no evil; for You are with me; Your rod and Your staff, they comfort me.

Psalm 34:18: The Lord is close to the brokenhearted and saves those who are crushed in spirit.

Psalm 94:19: When my anxious thoughts multiply within me, thy consolations delight my soul.

Psalm 147:3: He heals the brokenhearted and binds up their wounds.

Isaiah 25:8: He will swallow up death forever, and the Lord God will wipe away tears from all faces; The rebuke of His people He will take away from all the earth; For the Lord has spoken.

Isaiah 40:29-31: He gives power to the weak, and to those who have no might He increases strength. Even the youths shall faint and be weary, and the young men shall utterly fall, but those who wait on the Lord shall renew their strength; they shall mount up with wings like eagles, they shall run and not be weary, they shall walk and not faint.

Isaiah 49:13: Sing, O heavens! Be joyful, O earth! And break out in singing, O mountains! For the Lord has comforted His people, and will have mercy on His afflicted.

Isaiah 66:2: For all those things My hand has made, and all those things exist," says the Lord. "But on this one will I look on him who is poor and of a contrite spirit, and who trembles at My word.

Nehemiah 8: 10: Then he said to them, "Go your way, eat the fat, drink the sweet, and send portions to those for whom nothing is prepared; for this day is holy to our Lord. Do not sorrow, for the joy of the Lord is your strength."

John 14:18: I will not leave you orphans; I will come to you.

John 14:1-3: Let not your heart be troubled; you believe in God, believe also in Me. In My Father's house are many mansions; if it were not so, I would have told you. I go to prepare a place for you. And if I go and prepare a place for you, I will come again and receive you to Myself; that where I am, there you may be also.

Romans 8:28: And we know that in all things God works for the good of those who love him, who have been called according to his purpose.

2 Corinthians 1:3-4: Blessed be the God and Father of our Lord Jesus Christ, the Father of mercies and God of all comfort, who comforts us in all our tribulation, that we may be able to comfort those who are in any trouble, with the comfort with which we ourselves are comforted by God.

2 Thessalonians 2:16-17: Now may our Lord Jesus Christ Himself, and our God and Father, who has loved us and given us everlasting consolation and good hope by grace, comfort your hearts and establish you in every good word and work.

Matthew 5:4: Blessed are they that mourn: for they shall be comforted.

Revelation 21:4: And God will wipe away every tear from their eyes; there shall be no more death, nor sorrow, nor crying. There shall be no more pain, for the former things have passed away."

Practice Exercise #13:

Angeline L. Williams

For Times of Loneliness

Here are some of my favorite scriptures for times of loneliness. Some are commands, and some are promises. Meditate on these passages. Ask the Holy Spirit to help you understand the ones that stand out to you. Use these scriptures and others that come to mind and write down a couple of prayer confessions in the lesson in this section declaring your faith in God to settle you, and surround you with love. Keep in mind that no promise or scripture will help you if you don't put it into action. If the passage is a command do what it says. Don't worry about it, pray about it. God always keeps His promises.

Deuteronomy 4:31: For the LORD your God is a compassionate God; He will not fail you nor destroy you nor forget the covenant with your fathers which He swore to them.

Deuteronomy 31:6: Be strong and courageous, do not be afraid or tremble at them, for the LORD your God is the one who goes with you. He will not fail you or forsake you.

Deuteronomy 33:27: The eternal God is a dwelling place, and underneath are the everlasting arms; and He drove out the enemy from before you, and said, 'Destroy!'

Samuel 12:22: For the LORD will not abandon His people on account of His great name, because the LORD has been pleased to make you a people for Himself.

Isaiah 41:10: Do not fear, for I am with you; do not anxiously look about you, for I am your God. I will strengthen you, surely I will help you, surely I will uphold you with My righteous right hand.

Isaiah 43:1-2: Fear not, for I have redeemed you; I have called you by your name; You are Mine. When you pass through the waters, I will be with you; and through the rivers, they shall not overflow you. When you walk through the fire, you shall not be burned, nor shall the flame scorch you."

Isaiah 54:10: 'For the mountains may be removed and the hills may shake, but My loving kindness will not be removed from you, and My covenant of peace will not be shaken,' Says the LORD who has compassion on you.

Psalms 27:10: For my father and my mother have forsaken me, but the LORD will take me up. Psalms 46:1: GOD is our refuge and strength, a very present help in trouble.

Psalms 147:3: He heals the brokenhearted and binds up their wounds.

Psalm 139:7-10: Where can I go from Your Spirit? Or where can I flee from Your presence? If I ascend into heaven, You are there; if I make my bed in hell, behold, You are there. If I take the wings of the morning, and dwell in the uttermost parts of the sea, even there Your hand shall lead me, and Your right hand shall hold me."

Matthew 28:20: Teaching them to observe all that I commanded you; and lo, I am with you always, even to the end of the age.

John 14:1: Do not let your heart be troubled; believe in God, believe also in Me.

John 14:18: I will not leave you as orphans; I will come to you.

Romans 8:38-39: For I am convinced that neither death, nor life, nor angels, nor principalities, nor things present, nor things to come, nor powers, nor height, nor depth, nor any other created thing, will be able to separate us from the love of God, which is in Christ Jesus our Lord.

Romans 8:35-37: Who will separate us from the love of Christ? Will tribulation, or distress, or persecution, or famine, or nakedness, or peril, or sword? But in all these things we overwhelmingly conquer through Him who loved us

Practice Exercise #14:

Promises, Promises. God Always Keeps His Promises

For, Stress, Worry and Anxiety

Here are some scriptures and promises to combat stress, worry and anxiety. Some are commands, and some are promises. Meditate on these passages. Ask the Holy Spirit to help you understand the ones that stand out to you. Use these scriptures and others that come to mind and write down a couple of prayer confessions in the lesson in this section declaring your faith in God to surround you with His peace. Keep in mind that no promise or scripture will help you if you don't put it into action. If the passage is a command do what it says. Don't worry about it, pray about it. God always keeps His promises.

Genesis 15:1: After these things the word of the LORD came unto Abram in a vision, saying, Fear not, Abram: I am thy shield, and thy exceeding great reward.

Deuteronomy 20:3-4: And he shall say to them, 'Hear, O Israel: Today you are on the verge of battle with your enemies. Do not let your heart faint, do not be afraid, and do not tremble or be terrified because of them; for the Lord your God is He who goes with you, to fight for you against your enemies, to save you.'

Deuteronomy 31:6: Be strong and of a good courage, fear not, nor be afraid of them: for the LORD thy God, he it is that doth go with thee; he will not fail thee, nor forsake thee.

Joshua 1:9: Have I not commanded you? Be strong and of good courage; do not be afraid, nor be dismayed, for the Lord your God is with you wherever you go.

1 Chronicles 28:20: And David said to Solomon his son, Be strong and of good courage, and do it: fear not, nor be dismayed: for the LORD God, even my God, will be with thee; he will not fail thee, nor forsake thee, until thou hast finished all the work for the service of the house of the LORD.

2 Chronicles 20:17: You will not need to fight in this battle. Position yourselves, stand still and see the salvation of the Lord, who is with you, O Judah and Jerusalem!' Do not fear or be dismayed; tomorrow go out against them, for the Lord is with you."

Psalm 46:1-3: God is our refuge and strength, a very present help in trouble. Therefore we will not fear, though the earth should change and though the mountains slip into the heart of the sea; though its waters roar and foam, though the mountains quake at its swelling pride.

Psalm 91:1-2: He who dwells in the shelter of the Most High will abide in the shadow of the Almighty. I will say to the LORD, 'My refuge and my fortress, My God, in whom I trust!'

Psalm 121:1-8: I will lift up my eyes to the mountains; from whence shall my help come? My help comes from the LORD, who made heaven and earth. He will not allow your foot to slip; He who keeps you will not slumber. Behold, He who keeps Israel will neither slumber nor sleep.

Isaiah 26:3: You will keep him in perfect peace, whose mind is stayed on You, Because he trusts in You.

Isaiah 35:4: Say to them that are of a fearful heart, Be strong, fear not: behold, your God will come with vengeance, even God with a recompence; he will come and save you.

Isaiah 41:13: For I the LORD thy God will hold thy right hand, saying unto thee, Fear not; I will help thee.

Matthew 6:26: Look at the birds of the air, that they do not sow, nor reap nor gather into barns, and yet your heavenly Father feeds them. Are you not worth much more than they?

Matthew 6:34-35: Your heavenly Father knows that you have need of all these things. But seek ye first the kingdom of God, and his righteousness; and all these things shall be added unto you.

Romans 8:6: For the mind set on the flesh is death, but the mind set on the Spirit is life and peace.

Philippians 4:4: Rejoice in the Lord always: and again I say, Rejoice.

Philippians 4:6: Be anxious for nothing, but in everything by prayer and supplication with thanksgiving let your requests be made known to God.

Philippians 4:6-7: ⁶ Be anxious for nothing, but in everything by prayer and supplication, with thanksgiving, let your requests be made known to God; ⁷ and the peace of God, which surpasses all understanding, will guard your hearts and minds through Christ Jesus..

Philippians 4:8: Finally, brethren, whatever things are true, whatever things are noble, whatever things are just, whatever things are pure, whatever things are lovely, whatever things are of good report, if there is any virtue and if there is anything praiseworthy—meditate on these things.

Philippians 4:19: And my God will supply all your needs according to His riches in glory in Christ Jesus.

1 Peter 5:6-7: Therefore humble yourselves under the mighty hand of God, that He may exalt you in due time, casting all your care upon Him, for He cares for you.

Colossians 3:15: Let the peace of Christ rule in your hearts, to which indeed you were called in one body; and be thankful.

Angeline L. Williams

Practice Exercise #15:

Promises, Promises. God Always Keeps His Promises

Angeline L. Williams

When Things Get Tough

Trusting God is a choice to have faith in what He says even when your feelings or circumstances would have you believe something different. ignoring your feelings or reality does not mean that you are trusting God. Trusting God means believing in His dependability, His Word, His ability, and His strength. Circumstances can change in an instant, but God does not change. He is the same yesterday, today, and tomorrow and therefore is worthy of your trust. What He's done in the past, He can do again. What He's done for others, He can do for you.

Here are some verses to encourage you to trust God when things get tough. Some are commands, and some are promises. Meditate on these passages. Ask the Holy Spirit to help you understand the ones that stand out to you. Use these scriptures and others that come to mind and write down a couple of prayer confessions in the lesson in this section declaring your faith in God to answer your prayer. Keep in mind that no promise or scripture will help you if you don't put it into action. If the passage is a command do what it says. Don't worry about it, pray about it. God always keeps His promises.

Exodus 33:14: My presence will go with you, and I will give you rest.

Deuteronomy 31:8: It is the Lord who goes before you. He will be with you; he will not fail you or forsake you. Do not fear or be dismayed.

Deuteronomy 33:27: The eternal God is your refuge, and underneath are the everlasting arms.

Proverbs 3:5-6: Trust in the LORD with all your heart and do not lean on your own understanding. In all your ways acknowledge him, and he will direct your paths.

Psalm 9:10: Those who know Your name will put their trust in You, for You, O LORD, have not forsaken those who seek You.

Psalms 20:7: Some trust in chariots, and some in horses: but we will remember the name of the LORD our God.

Psalm 25:3-5: Indeed, none of those who wait for You will be ashamed; those who deal treacherously without cause will be ashamed. Make me know Your ways, O LORD; teach me Your paths. Lead me in Your truth and teach me, for You are the God of my salvation; for You I wait all the day.

Psalm 25:20: O my God, in You I trust, do not let me be ashamed; do not let my enemies exult over me.

Psalms 27:5: For in the day of trouble He will conceal me in His tabernacle; in the secret place of His tent He will hide me; He will lift me up on a rock.

Psalm 31:14: As for me, I trust in You, O LORD, I say, 'You are my God.'

Psalm 34:4: Delight yourself also in the LORD; and he will give you the desires of your heart.

Psalm 37:3-5: Trust in the Lord, and do good; dwell in the land, and feed on His faithfulness. Delight yourself also in the Lord, and He shall give you the desires of your heart. Commit your way to the Lord, trust also in Him, and He shall bring it to pass.

Psalm 34:17: When the righteous cry for help, the Lord hears, and rescues them from all their troubles.

Psalm 40:3-4: He put a new song in my mouth, a song of praise to our God; many will see and fear and will trust in the LORD. How blessed is the man who has made the LORD his trust, and has not turned to the proud, nor to those who lapse into falsehood.

Psalm 44:6: I will not trust in my bow, nor will my sword save me.

Psalm 52:8: As for me, I am like a green olive tree in the house of God; I trust in the lovingkindness of God forever and ever.

Psalm 56:3: When I am afraid, I will put my trust in You. In God, whose word I praise, in God I have put my trust; I shall not be afraid. What can mere man do to me?

Psalm 130:5-6: I wait for the LORD, my soul does wait, and in His word do I hope. My soul waits for the Lord more than the watchmen for the morning; indeed, more than the watchmen for the morning.

Psalm 145:14-15: The LORD sustains all who fall and raises up all who are bowed down. The eyes of all look to You, and You give them their food in due time.

Isaiah 26:4: Trust in the LORD forever, for in GOD the LORD, we have an everlasting Rock.

Hebrews 10:23: Let us hold fast the confession of our hope without wavering, for He who promised is faithful.

Habakkuk 2:3: For the vision is yet for the appointed time; it hastens toward the goal and it will not fail. Though it tarries, wait for it; for it will certainly come, it will not delay.

Lamentations 3:25-26: The LORD is good to those who wait for Him, to the person who seeks Him. It is good that he waits silently for the salvation of the LORD.

Luke 10:19: Behold, I give you the authority to trample on serpents and scorpions, and over all the power of the enemy, and nothing shall by any means hurt you.

Practice Exercise #16:

Promises, Promises. God Always Keeps His Promises

My Prayer for You

Heavenly Father, You are the God Who confirms the word of His servant, and performs the counsel of His messengers. (Isaiah 44:26) Father, I pray for me and every person who reads this word You have given me. Lord God let Your ear be attentive to the prayer of Your servant and to the prayer of Your servants who delight in revering Your name. Your servants dwell in the secret place of the Most High God, under the shadow of the Almighty. (Psalm 91:1) Our hearts are open to see Jesus Christ in the fullness of His glory. Pour out Your wisdom and revelation into our daily life.

You are the God who gives us the power to get wealth, that You may establish Your covenant, which You swore to our forefathers, as it is this day (Deuteronomy 8:18). Thank You for the power to get wealth that Your covenant might be established. Give us success today by granting us favor. Thank You that Your grace, blessing, and earthly favor abounds to us, so our needs are met, and we might be able to be a blessing to Your Kingdom.

Father, You are a Waymaker. You go before us pre-paring the way, making everything crooked straight, and every rough path smooth. Because of You we can walk in abundance in every area, with no exception. The Light of Christ breaks through the darkness and shines in our life so that You may be glorified. I declare we have the mind of Christ. The Sword of the Spirit guides and governs our thoughts to walk in the authority and dominion of Christ. We will seek things above, not beneath. We will cast down every thought that tries to exalt itself against God's word.

God's Truth protects our integrity. The shield of faith secures our destiny. Righteousness protects our reputation, and the Gospel of peace guides our every step. No weapon formed against us will prevail. We will refute every tongue that accuses us, for we are the righteousness of Christ. This is our heritage as servants of the Lord. We are justified by the Lord and established with honor and truth before all people. You have perfected all things concerning us.

Father, Your word is seed. Thank You that the seed and the dream You've planted in our hearts will grow, be fruitful, and multiply. You give us the desires of our hearts, and then You watch over the word to perform it (Psalm 37:4, Philippians 2:13). Your purposes and plans for our future will manifest in our life.

Father You supply seed to the sower and bread for food, and You increase our supply of seed and enlarge the harvest of our righteousness. (2 Corinthians 9:10, Luke 8:11). Fill our entire being (body, soul, and spirit) with the manifest presence of Your presence.

Thank You, Father, for surrounding us with Your favor and covering us like a shield. May all who see us look upon us with favor. We are blessed to be a blessing. Victorious is our way of life. Whatever we set our hands to that is conducive for God's purpose and plan for our life is blessed and prosperous. Let everything the enemy has stolen from us be returned according to Your word in Joel 2:25. Every misaligned thing in our life come into divine alignment in the name of Jesus.

So it has been spoken! So it shall be done in Jesus' name!

Notes

Write down the names of people you are praying for, or any notes, or things God has spoken to you.

_____
_____
_____
_____
_____
_____
_____
_____
_____
_____
_____
_____
_____

Angeline L. Williams

Promises, Promises. God Always Keeps His Promises

Angeline L. Williams

About The Author

Prophetess Angeline L. Williams is an author, speaker, Bible teacher. She has accepted her assignment to speak the truth with boldness and transparency. She was licensed and ordained in 2002 to preach the Gospel. She is a submitted vessel of God who flows in the ministry gifts of prophet, evangelist, and teacher.

Her passion for God and His Word has led to an anointing to preach and teach the word of God with authority, revelation, and deliverance. Her passion is to encourage and empower others to live a God-inspired life that far exceeds their limits. Her messages are illuminated with revelation, personal testimony and a depth of wisdom, and insight resulting from decades of study, and relationship with God.

She is also the author of Put The Word In Your Mouth: Believe God, Agree With His Word, Declare His Word, and Change Your Life! and I Don't Believe in Fairytales:

Breaking Anti-Marriage. She is the owner of Williams DocuPrep, where she has been providing self-publishing services to authors, and independent publishers since 2005. Visit her website at www.williamsdocuprep.com to learn more.

Prophetess Angeline is available to speak at churches, groups, conferences, workshops, and anywhere else God opens a door. Contact her about speaking at your event visit her website at: www.angelinelwilliams.com

"Let us not become weary in doing good, for at the proper time we will reap a harvest if we do not give up." — *Galatians 6:9*

There is so much more that I would love to share that will help you walk in the victory of Christ that it would take several books, so I invite you to follow me on my blog at: www.angelinelwilliams.com.

Join me on Facebook:
www.facebook.com/angeline.williams

Follow me on Twitter:
twitter.com/MsAngelineW

Other Books By Author
Available online where books are sold.

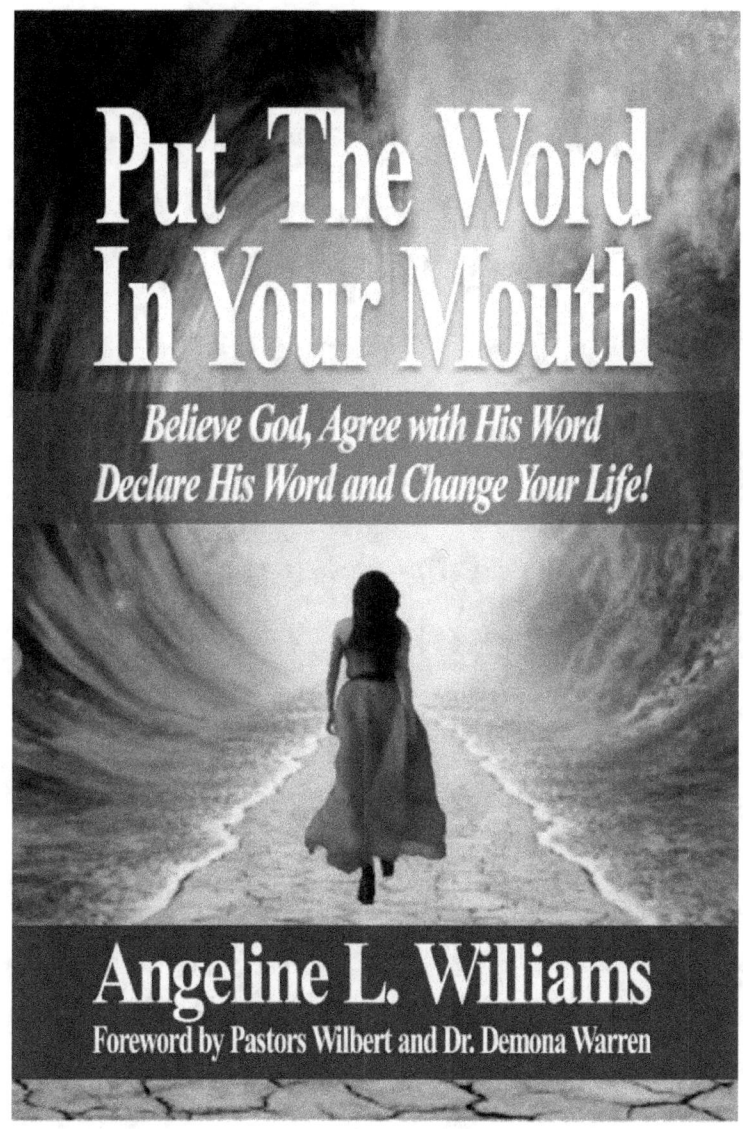

Promises, Promises. God Always Keeps His Promises

www.ingramcontent.com/pod-product-compliance
Lightning Source LLC
Chambersburg PA
CBHW071241070526
44583CB00017B/2281